AMERICAN HERITAGE
ILLUSTRATED HISTORY
OF THE UNITED STATES

Billiards was advertised in 1882 as a game suitably genteel for ladies.
NEW YORK HISTORICAL SOCIETY; BELLA C. LANDAUER COLLECTION

FRONT COVER: *The family of William Astor was painted by Lucius Rossi in 1875 in its Fifth Avenue mansion, which is now the site of the Empire State Building.*
COLLECTION OF MRS. VINCENT ASTOR

FRONT ENDSHEET: *J.B. Brewster & Company of 25th Street, New York City, advertised one of its coaches by means of this late 19th-century lithograph.*
NEW YORK HISTORICAL SOCIETY: BELLA C. LANDAUER COLLECTION

CONTENTS PAGE: *In 1878, Currier and Ives lampooned the pretensions of those with their coaches-and-four who drove about on a Sunday to see and be seen.*
MUSEUM OF THE CITY OF NEW YORK: HARRY T. PETERS COLLECTION

BACK ENDSHEET: *The family of William Astor was painted by Lucius Rossi in 1875 in its Fifth Avenue mansion, which stood where the Empire State Building now is. From left to right: Daughter Helen; William, grandson of John Jacob Astor I; daughter Gussie; John Jacob Astor IV, who was lost in the sinking of the* Titanic; *Mrs. William (nee Caroline Schermerhorn); and daughter Caroline.*
COLLECTION OF MRS. VINCENT ASTOR

BACK COVER: *Society promenades (top) in the Waldorf Hotel in this nineteenth-century millinery poster; the famed showman P. T. Barnum (bottom left) is seen presenting tiny Tom Thumb and his wife to Queen Victoria in this mid nineteenth-century lithograph; Mark Twain (bottom right) gave the period its name, the Gilded Age.*
AMERICAN ANTIQUARIAN SOCIETY: NEW YORK HISTORICAL SOCIETY: MARK TWAIN MEMORIAL, HARTFORD, CONNECTICUT

AMERICAN HERITAGE ILLUSTRATED HISTORY OF THE UNITED STATES

VOLUME 11

THE GILDED AGE

BY ROBERT G. ATHEARN

Created in Association with the
Editors of AMERICAN HERITAGE

and for the updated edition
MEDIA PROJECTS INCORPORATED

CHOICE PUBLISHING, INC.
New York

Library of Congress Catalog Card Number: 87-73399
ISBN 0-945260-11-3
ISBN 0-945260-00-8

This 1988 edition is published and distributed by Choice Publishing, Inc., 53 Watermill Lane, Great Neck, NY 11021 by arrangement with American Heritage, a division of Forbes, Inc.

Manufactured in the United States of America
10 9 8 7 6 5 4

CONTENTS OF THE COMPLETE SERIES

Editor's Note to the Revised Edition
Introduction by ALLAN NEVINS
Main text by ROBERT G. ATHEARN

EACH VOLUME CONTAINS AN ENCYCLOPEDIC SECTION; MASTER INDEX IN VOLUME 18

COACHING. FOUR IN HAND.
A Swell Turn-out.

CONTENTS OF VOLUME 11

CHAPTER 31

WEALTH AND ITS WORLD

I worship in the church of the libertines." This was the alleged boast of "Jubilee Jim" Fisk in the year 1869. He was a fat and flamboyant man, who loved to dress in uniforms awash with braid, or drive costly rigs down New York's avenues with expensive and lovely women beside him. Only a few years before the Civil War, Fisk was peddling gimcracks from a wagon in New England's countryside. He pyramided his profits by shrewd dealings in war-scarce commodities. He bought his way into steamship lines, then railroads, and finally became one of an infamous trio directing the fortunes of the Erie. Together with Daniel Drew, a thin ex-cattledrover, and Jay Gould, once an upstate New York store clerk, Fisk used the Erie's treasury to float loans, promote get-rich-quick schemes, and drive the stock market up and down for pleasure and profit. In fact, Drew, Fisk, and Gould appeared to use Erie's money for any purpose other than the improvement and operation

Situated at Wall and Broad Streets in 1882, J. P. Morgan's company was close to the New York Stock Exchange (center).

of the railroad. Fisk in particular used it unabashedly on himself, his girls, and such little hobbies as buying the colonelcy of a militia regiment or building an opera house. His frank boast of being a libertine struck a new note in a once-frugal and self-improving America. His kind put the gilding on the Gilded Age.

Yet Fisk was probably not typical of the new America that was emerging as Ulysses S. Grant took over the Presidency in 1869. And, in fact, the Gilded Age is one of those loose descriptive jackets that can fit any period in general, and therefore no period in particular. The name comes from a novel by Mark Twain and Charles Dudley Warner, published in 1873, aimed primarily at lampooning lobbyists, swindlers, politicians whose price tags showed, and those who had got rich quickly and easily in the postwar boom. Yet underneath the tinsel were the solid facts of industrial production, expansion westward, urban growth, and immigration. Millions of Americans lived and worked without ever building an expensive home, taking a "grand tour" to Europe, or turning over a share of stock.

William K. Vanderbilt had Richard Morris Hunt build him a chateau (left) on Fifth Avenue. Edward Harriman's house (right) was at 11 East 62nd Street.

The Gilded Age fades casually, in some books, into the Gay Nineties, but it is well to remember that the years from 1869 to 1900 knew strikes and depressions, bitterness and despair, as well as buoyancy and free-spending. In short, both the achievements and agonies of the years that bridge Appomattox and the new century are blurred by careless catchwords.

Nevertheless, it *is* true to say that wealth was the dominant fact of the period—the huge, overpowering overflow from mine and mill, forest and farm that made it possible for men to speak of millions as they had for-

merly spoken of thousands. Everything was on a more gigantic and more noticeable scale, including the lives of those who reaped most of the new riches. Certainly they were not all carbon copies of Jubilee Jim. Some of them strained, by works of piety, charity, and benevolence, to get through the needle's eye into the kingdom of heaven. Others, unable or unwilling to forget the parsimony of their boyhoods, went on working 16-hour days and reinvesting each surplus nickel, so that 10 factories might become 20 and one million become two. But whatever they did, their power was

The library of Jay Gould's house was ornately overfurnished, and in the best tradition of the Gilded Age, it had almost more knickknacks than books.

felt in society, and their behavior influenced other social classes. Their benefactions endowed churches and colleges, libraries and journals, and—just incidentally—political campaigns. It was no wonder that preachers and professors and editors and legislators all seemed to live in the shadow of the rich. The new nabobs set the tone.

A taste for ostentation

The very freedom with which they spent money on their physical surroundings left its mark on architecture. Leland Stanford and Charles Crocker, magnates of the Southern Pacific, lived on San Francisco's Nob Hill in mansions that bristled with bay windows, towers, cupolas, and pointed roofs, and whose interiors were crammed with French mirrors, Belgian carpeting, Gothic paneling, inlaid wood floors, and carved staircases. Surrounded by such niceties, and by paintings and tapestries brought wholesale from Europe, the new millionaires could reflect upon their long journey from unheated farmhouses and outdoor plumbing. Jay Cooke, "financier of the Civil War," also an alumnus of the countryside, dwelt in New York in a "vast

A dog show at Madison Square Garden in the early 1890s brought out the socially elite in their puffed-sleeve dresses and hats piled with flowers.

gloomy pile of granite, 175 feet long, with 72 rooms," whose cost was $2,000,000.

Yet men of presumed refinement could stumble, too. Bayard Taylor, traveler and poet, had an "Italian villa, its main body square and ugly," with "a tall tower, with spire, dormer windows, and a veranda in it." As one author has noted, a "mania for the grandiose" seized on builders. "Monsters of shingle crawled upon suburban lawns." All of this extravagance was in part due to an ebullient pride of possession, and in part to a yearn-

ing for filling space with details. This came naturally to a people who had just filled an almost empty continent. Perhaps, too, they were symbolically trying to cram content into empty places in their spirits, suddenly revealed to them by their new leisure. At any rate, the interiors of wealthy and middle-class residences alike reflect a stupefying profusion of chairs, end tables, ottomans, lamps, curtains, "throws," shelves, and knickknacks.

American dress also revealed that this was an era of plenty. Women dutifully followed styles popularized by Empress Eugenie during the '60s, right down to the horizontally striped stockings, Zouave jackets, and Empire bonnets. In the '70s, there was an outburst of bustles. By the '90s, puffed sleeves, broad-brimmed hats laden with artificial birds and vegetation, and generous yards of skirt marked the woman whose husband had done well. As for the husbands themselves, black broadcloth was the sober garb for the office where the world was properly managed, but stovepipe hats were acceptable, and a brocaded vest, a gold chain, and even a diamond stickpin were permitted to some of the solidest citizens.

The styles of spending affected by the successful families of the day were not entirely uniform, however. Even among the great names there were distinctions. Andrew Carnegie, the steel baron, lived well, but his expansive moods were fulfilled in private railroad cars and castles in Scotland rather than by ornately decorating his American mansions. John D. Rockefeller lived in homes in Cleveland and New York that were rich but not gaudy. Indeed, as the '80s and '90s brought with them a wave of protest against trusts and plutocrats, the men of genuine wealth tended to seek retirement from the public eye, often abroad. The role of public sport was left to the second-line millionaires—newspaper owners like James Gordon Bennett, Jr., an expert in Parisian restaurants and race tracks; or star salesmen, like "Diamond Jim" Brady; or miners who had not lost the ripsnorting vigor of the Wild West, like Denver's H. A. W. Tabor, who built a million-dollar opera house in the Rockies and allegedly blustered that Shakespeare's portrait in the lobby should give way to his own, for, after all, "What the hell has Shakespeare done for Denver?"

Politicos of note

The impact of big business on politics was measured not merely in legislation, but in the lives of the politicians themselves. They, too, bore a well-fed look, and the more noteworthy among them lived in a style befitting their new grandeur. (As the Speaker of the House, Maine's Thomas B. Reed, remarked in 1890, the United States was now a "billion-dollar country.") When he traveled, Michigan's Senator-boss Zachariah Chandler had liveried servants to attend him, with a prominent letter C worked into their coattails in embroidery. "Zack" was already a wealthy Detroit merchant, and thus foreshadowed the later period (at the end of the '90s and in the first decade of the 20th century) when tycoons would "retire" to the Senate to keep an eye on the country and permit their wives to mingle in Washington society. Among such members of the "millionaires' club" were mining barons like George Hearst of California, coal and iron kings like Mark Hanna of Ohio, lumbermen like Wisconsin's Philetus Sawyer. It was not too hard to buy a Senate seat when state legislatures did the electing, as was the case until 1913.

Of equal interest were the kingmakers in city, state, and national politics who made their fortunes almost entirely by their political activities. High in the Republican firmament, from 1876 onward, rode the star of James Gillespie Blaine of Maine. Blaine had been, briefly, a schoolteacher and editor before find-ing his way into and around legislative halls. Affable, popular, and influential, he soon became the most notable Republican in the House and then the Senate. Years gave him a well-padded belly, testimony to many sumptuous dinners in an era that considered it insulting not to offer eight or 10 courses—soup, fish, game, roasts, vegetables, fruits, cheeses, puddings, cakes, and ices—at one sitting. Blaine

A cartoon in the 1884 Presidential campaign attacks "Grover the Good" for his illegitimate child. The caption reads, "Another voice for Cleveland."

910

A caricature of a then-popular French painting has Republican Presidential candidate James G. Blaine tattooed with his crimes and revealed before his party.

lived not ostentatiously but most comfortably in several homes, on salaries which had been set low in an earlier day that distrusted paid public servants. This discrepancy between income and outgo was not particularly remarked on until it was revealed that Blaine had been handsomely treated by certain railroads in the way of fees and commissions, and that he had been assiduous in helping out those same railroads in Congress. The damning evidence, contained in a packet of letters, was not enough to get Blaine indicted for anything—and he probably was no more venal than most of his contemporaries by the easygoing standards of the time. But enough taint clung to him to make reformers distrustful. For orthodox party orators, Blaine was "The Plumed Knight"; for the doubtful, he remained the tattooed man. His genial willingness to use public position for private benefit was as surely a stamp of politics in his time as were his beard and his volumes of orations on the grandeurs of the Union and the Republican Party.

Blaine was involved in two major political duels, both of which shine further light on political styles in the

Richard Croker, the head of New York's political world, is mocked by the cartoonist as the sun around which revolve his many corrupt satellites.

years from U. S. Grant to William McKinley. Within the Republican Party until 1881, his most distinguished enemy was New York's Senator Roscoe Conkling. A gorgeous, bearded six-foot figure, who dressed like a swell and acted like a proconsul, Conkling had once provoked Blaine to comment on his "turkey-gobbler strut." The two men disliked each other, and fought bitterly at conventions and elsewhere, as chieftains of two factions—the Half Breeds (Blaine's men) and the Stalwarts.

Blaine won that battle finally, but it is significant that Conkling then turned easily and successfully back to a career as a railroad and corporation lawyer. And it was Conkling who got into the courts the argument that the Fourteenth Amendment was deliberately intended to protect corporations, as "persons," from abridgment of their "privileges"—that is, regulation—by the states. Some thought the amendment was talking only about blacks and their immunities from state harassment, but Conkling said

912

he had been on the drafting committee and knew differently! In the long run, he may have had more influence on American history than Blaine.

Then, in 1884, Blaine managed to obtain the Presidential nomination, which pitted him against New York's Governor Grover Cleveland and launched American history's most lurid campaign up to then. High-minded Republicans, in droves, deserted Blaine as the symbol of a boss-controlled candidate, bound hand and foot to big business. They preferred the Democrat Cleveland, a huge pillar of a man whose economic philosophy was conservative—no handouts to business, labor, the farmer, or indeed anyone—and who was as honest and independent as George Washington was. These proper Republican "mugwumps" got the shock of their lives, however, when it was disclosed that Cleveland, as a sportive young bachelor lawyer in Buffalo, had fathered a child out of wedlock. Here was a dreadful choice: Blaine, whose private life was apparently exemplary, had come close—too close—to violating the accepted public morality of the time. Cleveland, on the other hand, had violated the Victorian code that made a man caught in a private immoral act unfit for "decent" society. One wit suggested that the obvious solution was to retire Blaine to the private life he so well adorned, and elevate Cleveland to the public office he kept so scrupulously honorable. While the voters pondered this choice, rallies of Republicans shouted, "Ma, Ma, where's my pa? Gone to the White House, ha, ha, ha!" and rallies of Democrats shouted, "Blaine, Blaine, James G. Blaine, continental liar from the state of Maine!" The election went to Cleveland by a close margin, but what the victory signified, historians are still not agreed on.

City bosses and "coarse" politics

Victorian was used to describe the morality of the last three decades of the 19th century. It is a word not wholly appropriate, as its origin is English, and although the respectable classes in America were much like their English counterparts, there was always enough difference in American types and tastes to keep the similar groups from quite matching. Still, guardians of propriety in both countries were identically Victorian in refusing to recognize whatever they regarded as "coarse." Among American Victorian politicians, therefore, certain city bosses stand out in bold relief by their triumphant coarseness. The best known of these, because of the extraordinary publicity he received, was New York's William Marcy Tweed, the son of an English cabinetmaker, who became master of Tammany Hall and then of the city in the late '60s. Tweed had been a roughneck as a youngster, winning his following with his fists and liberal treats of drink. He never tried to mask his origins. When he and his ring got control of New York's board of aldermen and City Hall, and made for themselves millions of dollars in selling licenses, franchises, and contracts, Tweed blew it grandiosely and with vulgar glee. Threatened with exposure, he simply growled, "What are you going to do about it?" and when it turned out that reformers were able to put him in jail about it, he died unrepentant. Styles in bosses change, however. Twenty years after Tweed, the keeper of the Tammany tiger was Richard Croker. His shakedowns from the underworld were collected neatly and systematically by lieutenants. He cut himself in, properly and legally, on the overpriced contracts for municipal improvement that his puppets in the city administration approved. And from time to time he retired with his take to an estate in Ireland, where he raised blooded horses like a gentleman. (After 1901, when the reformers made New York too hot for him, he stayed there.) Even the boss was gradually becoming a little less gaudy.

Blaine, Tweed, and Croker notwithstanding, there *were* honest politicians. Upright men held Congressional seats, sat in cabinets, and even ran for the Presidency—like old glue and iron manufacturer Peter Cooper, Greenback Party candidate in 1876, or one of the heroes of Gettysburg, General Winfield Scott Hancock, who carried the Democratic banner in 1880, but unfortunately had little to recommend him beyond honesty. Figures like Massachusetts Senator George Hoar, or Missouri's Carl Schurz, who was Secretary of the Interior under Rutherford B. Hayes, appear on the scene here and there like ancestral portraits frowning stiffly from the walls at the younger set's wild parties. But the men who made the political headlines of the day either had, or served, or were shaped by wealth and power. They had spacious ambitions, large appetites, and, all too often, small consciences.

Men of God

The heavy, ornamented, grandiose mark of the age was also on churches where the "arrived" worshiped. By the 1870s, Boston, New York, and Philadelphia had their fashionable preachers like Phillips Brooks, Theodore Cuyler, and T. DeWitt Talmage. But perhaps the most representative figure of all was the pastor of Plymouth Church in Brooklyn—Henry Ward Beecher. He was distinguished by his enormous popularity and by his skillful handling of the explosive issue of Darwinism. When evolution began to make its way into popular thought, its clear denial of the time scheme of the Old Testament (taken literally) was a shock to many churches. Rural parsonages and pewholders would have none of it. But sophisticated and well-off urban audiences were ready for an interpretation that would reconcile the God of their fathers with the science they so respected. (They respected it because its child, technology, was building so many marvels around them.) Beecher

"TO THEE I CLING."

In the storm of scandals breaking around him, Henry Ward Beecher hangs on to life by clinging to his Plymouth Church congregation and to his salary.

told his wealthy congregation, composed of businessmen with "suburban" homes in Brooklyn, that the God of Genesis was also the God of evolution. He had labored for eons, not days, and made the mighty, revolving cosmos as a testament to His creative power. He had brought man upward from primeval ooze to man's present noble and mighty estate, and all as a token of His love. Disdaining clerical garb or a pulpit, he stood before his audience looking like one of them, and told them in rich prose that God adored them, had made the universe for them, and now they could go home to enjoy their dinners.

The irony in all this was that Beecher was the descendant of a long line of Calvinist preachers who insisted that

915

man was a worm, justly doomed to hell-fire. Emotional and sensitive, Henry Ward revolted against his background, reveled in flowers, music, jewels, and the privileges that a huge income from lecturing and writing brought him. Then, in 1874, his ardent nature seemed to have doomed him. He became involved in a scandal over his relationship with the wife of one of his parishioners, Theodore Tilton, who took him to court. The trial was a national sensation and resulted in a hung jury. It is noteworthy that Beecher's congregation never lost faith in him, and that his popularity remained undimmed until his death, several years later. The Gilded Age would tolerate much in its prophets; it would put up with Beecher's alleged (but never quite proven) immorality, just as in another way it permitted Robert G. Ingersoll to remain an honored lawyer even while he shocked the pious everywhere by lectures espousing agnosticism. After all, his

ideas might be heretical, but he was a Union veteran, a Republican, a good family man, and a distinguished attorney; he ate heartily and spoke fluently. What more could be required?

Another titan of the age, in his way, was a lay preacher with a far different outlook from Beecher's. Dwight Lyman Moody also believed that God loved the world—so much, indeed, that He had given His son, that whosoever believed in Him should be saved. But Moody's God was not the God of evolution; rather, he was the God of the Holy Scriptures, self-pronouncing, who had appeared to Abraham, Moses, Jeremiah, and Saul of Tarsus and dealt with them in their palpable flesh. Moody, barely literate, came off a Massachusetts farm, where he was born in 1837. He went to Boston, then Chicago, where he be-

The peace and the beauty of this camp meeting painted in 1874 by Worthington Whittredge seem far distant from the phrenetic revival sessions held during the same period by Dwight Lyman Moody.

came a successful commission salesman, on the way to a business career. Nevertheless, during the Civil War he threw over his future in the marketplace and set about winning souls. He organized Sunday schools and missions, then took to the road himself in the '70s and '80s, with his organist and singer, Ira Sankey, to tell packed "tabernacles" the good news of salvation. The Old and New Testaments were literally true; men and women had only to affirm their belief in order to be made righteous; once the act of simple decision—of saying "I will" in answer to the question "Will you accept Christ?"—was taken, one would find it easy to forsake sin (the drunkard's cup, the gaming table, the lewd book, the broken Sabbath) and become a hard-working and churchgoing citizen, who need never beg for his bread in America. "A heart that is right with God seldom constitutes a social problem," said Moody.

Moody's apparently uncomplicated theology seemed to be out of step with the new era, but it was put over by hard work and large-scale organization. Publicity campaigns heralded his coming; choirs and ushers were trained and drilled for weeks before the meetings, and a neat touch was added by providing, around the main hall, "inquiry rooms" where those who had been reached by Moody's message could be privately counseled and prayed for by ministers after the service. In short, Moody was an empire builder in his own way. He never had trouble getting donations from big businessmen to carry on his work, even when they hardened their hearts against others who sought their help. And the reason was, as one of them put it, "He is one of us."

The ruddy-faced Beecher and the businesslike Moody were alike figures of the new, big-time religion. In the cities, the wealthy bought pews in "good" churches much as they held stock in sound corporations. Below them, the middling folk reared in a rural, Protestant mold sang Moody-and-Sankey hymns on Sunday, and dropped their nickels into the collection plate. Others among the urban masses either worshiped at Mass or in the synagogue, or were "lost" to the churches. In the hill country of the West and South, sinners rolled and shouted in the old-time agonies and ecstasies of the camp meeting. But the dominant note of the age in religion was bigness, tempered by sentimentality and evidenced by ornament. In religion, as in business and in politics, the upsurge of American success resulted in a culture that was in love with intricate display. It was almost baroque, except that it had no central idea or theme behind it, as the age of the baroque had. Leland Stanford could not, even in his palace, stand for what Louis XIV stood for; Moody could not be a Protestant pope (and how the idea would have horrified him!). But while it lasted, the Gilded Age gave hollow magnificence a local habitation and a name.

THE ROMANTIC WORLD
OF CURRIER AND IVES

The 19th century had no photographic or color magazines, few museums, and no movies or television, but it had one vastly popular art form through which today we can glimpse the spirit of that vanished time. The firm established by Nathaniel Currier in 1835, and joined by James Merritt Ives in 1857, has left behind a matchless record of the mid-1800s—the events, the people, and the lives they led—in the form of thousands of cheap, hand-colored lithographs. Once they sold new for 15¢ to $3; the hard-to-find ones today bring thousands of dollars. As this picture portfolio suggests, Currier and Ives overlooked little. News, places, heroes, elections, rural scenes, wars, disasters, popular humor, sad mottoes, inspirational scenes, and artful decorations—in sum, the tears and laughter of an age—were the specialties of the house.

"Those who labor in the earth," wrote Jefferson, "are the chosen people of God." Such was common American belief, reflected in this happy, well-scrubbed farm scene of 1853.

With the dawn of the Gilded Age, city people—in contrast to rural folk—began to live elegantly and ostentatiously. Here their carriages dash about New York's Central Park.

The Four Seasons of Life: Childhood is one of a Currier and Ives series portraying bucolic life as it surely never was. How impossibly neat and good these children are!

STURDY FARMERS, CITY SWELLS, AND THE PLEASANT SIDE OF LIFE IN AMERICA

This skater in ermine tippet, muff, and trim —described as *The Belle of the Winter* by the printmakers—is a mid-Victorian glamour girl.

Unless otherwise credited, all Currier and Ives prints in this portfolio are from the Collection of Harry T. Peters at the Museum of the City of New York.

Idyllic views of places dear to American hearts were a Currier and Ives best-seller. Above is the home of the author Washington Irving, Sunnyside, on the Hudson, and below is that same busy, placid river winding alongside West Point, as it was in 1861.

THE NATION'S PRIDE

A celestial cloud enveloping George Washington, with the national Capitol above and Mount Vernon below—and there is a typical patriotic print, suitable for framing.

SENTIMENT RAN THICK

Currier and Ives knew how much their audience admired the tender sentiments of love and produced them by the yard. The flowers at left are called *The Lady's Bouquet*. They were only the adult version of what the beauty who has won *The Little Beau* (below) received as a token of his affection. The old favorite at the right carries love back to the more adult level and is titled *Kiss Me Quick*.

WE MET BY CHANCE; OR WAITING FOR THE SWELL

THE HEIGHT
OF
LOW COMEDY

Prim, pathos-loving, and occasionally downright mournful, the Victorian Age could also laugh, genteelly or uproariously. Currier and Ives went in heavily for comics, of which a sampling is shown here. No great gulf seems to separate jokes of this variety from those of the space age—and then, as now, girls seem to play a big part. As Artemus Ward, the humorist of that era, put it, "The female woman is one of the greatest institooshuns of which this land can boast." The bear seems to think so, too.

WHICH DONKEY SHALL I TAKE?

HUG ME CLOSER, GEORGE

THE MORAL EXHORTERS

The late Victorians, followers of Horatio Alger and inheritors of *Poor Richard's Almanac,* took morality seriously and liked to hang mottoes to remind themselves of their duties. These two examples outline the routes, respectively, to Heaven and Wealth.

HED BY CURRIER & IVES   Copyright, 1875 by Currier & Ives, N.Y.   125 NASSAU ST. NEW YORK

THE LADDER OF FORTUNE.

ndustry and Morality bring solid rewards.   Idle schemes and speculations yield poverty and ruin

CHAPTER 32

THE CITY'S GIDDY WHIRL

You are going far away,
But remember what I say
When you are in the city's giddy whirl—
From temptations, crimes, and follies,
Buses, hansom cabs, and trolleys,
Heaven will protect the working girl.

Thus, in a popular ballad of the '90s, did a country mother warn her daughter of perils ahead in the mighty metropolis. For already the city was a place where sin was all too visible. Yet it is probable that many Little Nells shrugged off such counsels, packed their bags, and went down to become counter girls or "type writers" (as stenographers were then known) in Chicago or Boston or New York. The great rush to the city went on without abatement. In 1860, only one-sixth of all Americans lived in communities of 8,000 or more. By 1900, more than one-third of the population lived in what the census bureau defined as cities. Vast numbers of them were in a few king-size hives. When the five boroughs of Greater New York were consolidated in 1898,

On a 1901 magazine cover, a fashionably dressed sleighing party steps onto snow-covered Fifth Avenue just below 52nd Street.

they made it possible for the census takers, two years later, to number over 3,000,000 New Yorkers. Philadelphia, by 1900, had 1,300,000 souls, and Chicago, the gem of the prairie, 1,700,000.

The desire of farm boys and girls to see the city was not surprising. It was in the city that such comforts of life as indoor plumbing, central heating, theaters, libraries, and educational opportunities awaited. More than that, any list of millionaires would reveal a great preponderance of occupations in trade and transportation. Agriculture had no representatives here except, perhaps, for an occasional cattle king. The great desire of youth was to find a place in the industrial world and rise, someday, to the rank of captain of industry. The shriek of the factory whistle and the trolley's impatient clang were siren songs to the young Ulysses behind the plow (and to his sister as well). So the countryfolk deserted the old homestead by the thousands.

Once in the big town, the newcomer found himself in the midst of a scene that was madly, wildly changing. Within the last 25 years of the century, the city put on its modern look.

931

The first elevated railroad appeared in New York in 1878. It was steam-driven, noisy, and a ghastly fire hazard, but it was worshiped as progress and imitated. Horsecars had been around since the 1830s, but they were slow, jerky, and smelly. In 1887, in Richmond, Virginia, there was the first successful trial of a street rail-way powered by electricity, and the advantages of electric railways in the city—the blessed "electric," which emitted neither cinders nor manure (nor exhaust fumes, a modern reader may add)—were made plain. It took until the century's end to get New York's elevated lines converted to electricity, and by that time, the mon-

932

The pillar of light below was in the Palace of Electricity at the Columbian Exposition of 1893 in Chicago. It was studded with colored globes flashing out changing patterns that today would hardly be glanced at but were then so novel they held the public spellbound. The scene at the left is of Grand Street in lower New York City around 1890, after electric street lights had been installed, making it easier and safer to get about at night.

ster town was already digging a subway (which did not, however, open until 1904). Meanwhile, to accommodate streetcar tracks (among other things), cobblestones and asphalt replaced dirt on thousands of miles of the nation's streets. City children lost the pleasure of feeling the earth between their bare toes on a summer

933

day; on the other hand, they had joys denied to their country cousins. The circus came more often, and for those who liked them, there were museums and libraries. And city streets offered more interesting sights —crowds, fights, fallen horses, new buildings going up—than anything in a country town.

Other changes, too, were transforming the city as technology and engineering cut into time and space and darkness. Iron bridges raised their tracery of towers and arches over the Mississippi and New York's East River. St. Louis had a bridge by 1874. In 1883, the Brooklyn Bridge was opened amid wild celebration and fireworks. One of the first great suspension bridges, its sturdy uprights and heavy cables were a wonderful amalgam of art, science, and utility. Yet steam ferries continued to carry much of the commuter load in and out of Manhattan, even though the Williamsburg Bridge, also over the East River,

was completed and opened by 1903.

In 1879, the incandescent bulb was perfected by Thomas A. Edison. Even earlier, the Brush carbon arc lamp had given a flaring, greenish electric "light" to the streets of some cities. By 1890 or thereabouts, the more manageable Edison type of lamp was casting its glare over urban night scenes. Gas lamps held on in homes and streets for a long time; it was under them that the painted women lured the farm boys, according to Carl

In July, 1866, after several attempts, Cyrus Field financed a fleet of ships that set sail from southern Ireland, bound for Newfoundland, playing out a cable along the floor of the Atlantic. The fleet reached its destination on July 27, and since then there has been telegraphic communication across the ocean.

Sandburg's *Chicago.* By 1889, too, New York already had central power stations for transmitting electricity to wide areas, and was already undertaking the job of transferring electric wires underground. A jungle of over-

935

Today any player striking the pose of the shortstop (left) or the third baseman (right) would be strictly bush-league, but in 1882 the big leaguers did it this way.

head strands, carried on poles with six and eight crossarms, had grown up, and in a severe storm, collapsing poles and live wires were major hazards.

Telephone wires were involved also. The first workable Bell instrument had been shown at Philadelphia's Centennial Exposition in 1876. By 1901, there was a telephone for every 40 Americans—perhaps 2,000,000 of them, mostly concentrated in the cities. And the typewriter was finding its way into more and more offices. In 1900, Edgar Allan Poe might have written an urban version of *The Bells*

that incorporated the clang of the trolley bell, the jingle of the telephone, and the soft "ting" of the typewriter carriage reaching the end of a line. The city, in short, had its new look by the time a New York baby born in 1879 would be casting his first vote. He would walk to the polling place past masonry buildings, as many as 12 stories high, supported on steel frames; he might telephone a friend for an appointment, hop an "elevated," and after dinner walk along a Broadway that was already becoming the Gay White Way, aglitter with jewels of

936

electricity. If he cared to stay up late —to attend the theater, perhaps—he would learn that the new city was never wholly quiet, never all dark. Even in the smallest hours, policemen walked their beats, lights burned in the windows of factories pushing out a rush order, roisterers tottered homeward, and newsboys rushed down to the ferries with early editions, to catch the first officebound rush. America had gone to town, and found it a busy place.

Entertainers and educators

The city was developing characteristic institutions, too. It was the mother and nurse of a number of new institutions, which the fathers of the nation would hardly have recognized. There was, for example, the "new journalism." Newspapers had begun in America as political and commercial organs. Around 1835, a genius named James Gordon Bennett discovered the enormous potentialities of playing to the new metropolitan audience of workers and servants, who held neither property nor public office, never expected to, and did not care who did. They wanted to be entertained, and told, in a general way, what was going on in the great, noisy world around them. Actually, Bennett had had a few predecessors in the business of providing "cheap" papers, but his New York *Herald* was an almost unique creation, stamped with his own vigorous personality. It gave the established classes all the political,

UMPIRING MADE EASY.

A HINT FOR THE NEW YORK NINE.—GIVE THE UMPIRE A CHANCE.

Umpires in 1866 obviously were no more popular with the public than they are now.

commercial, and diplomatic news they could hold; it also supplied prizefight and police-court reports to titillate the curious; and finally it gave them plenty of Bennett's noisy, self-centered, shamelessly personal, and always interesting editorials. Five years after the *Herald* got under way, it was followed by the New York *Tribune,* whose chief figure, Vermonter Horace Greeley, was a violent uplifter who made his paper a great (but lively) bible of all reform movements. The New York *Times* came along in 1851. Other papers changed their formats or

937

The only shock in the "sensational" magazine of 1874 might well come from electricity. Here Claude, the cad, gets his.

followed the lead of the big three, and by 1860, daily papers with circulations of 60,000 were not uncommon.

The 1870s were years of breakthroughs, however. Technology made possible the use of illustrations, headlines, display advertising, and runs of hundreds of thousands daily. The Atlantic cable brought European news overnight. New editors reached out for fresh readers. Joseph Pulitzer, William R. Nelson, and Victor Lawson made the St. Louis *Post-Dispatch,* the Kansas City *Star,* and the Chicago *Daily News* models of a new breed. Their papers were larger; they were full of late news and large-type advertisements for every kind of urban necessity. Reporters were thrusting, persistent, nosy. They interviewed Presidents and opera stars, diplomats and convicted embezzlers, and ran the results under two- and three-column headlines. And they also poked into hidden places at city hall in search of graft, skulduggery, and "fix." Their editors knew there was gold in becoming the public snoops and consciences of a great city. They prodded the residents to clean up their lawns, establish parks, drive boodlers from government, improve the waterfronts, and make their home towns great. They also knew that a paper should entertain, and they filled their pages with humorous features, stories, and cartoons, all of which were being sold in many places at once by syndicates, thus nationalizing urban culture.

In New York, journalism of this kind was pioneered (after Bennett had retired and after Greeley died in 1872) by Charles A. Dana, who made of the relatively unknown *Sun* a spicy paper full of good, inquisitive, colorful, human reporting and of cynically liverish Dana-written editorials that respected no one. Then, in 1883, Joseph Pulitzer moved into town from St. Louis, bought up the nearly defunct little New York *World,* and stood journalism on its ear. Pulitzer was a Hungarian immigrant who had learned the tastes of the American masses to a T. He supplied them, through the *World,* with free picnics,

The New York Sun *issued this advertisement in the late 19th century when circulation was a million a week and daily delivery cost all of 50¢ a month.*

excursions, handouts, and stunts—like raising the fund, in schoolchildren's pennies, for the base of the Statue of Liberty. He also gave them sensational reporting, like young Elizabeth Cochrane's having herself committed to the city insane asylum for 10 days to expose its horrible conditions—from which she emerged with a major reputation for her by-line "Nellie Bly." In addition, Pulitzer crusaded vigorously against monopolies and the exertions of bosses in their behalf (though the years made him personally a millionaire like the very men he was attacking in his role of the people's champion). And to round out its coverage, the *World* had comic strips, color sections, drawings, a huge Sunday edition with the latest from the world of sports and fashions, women's columns full of advice on how to hold a job or a mate—in short, something for everyone, always served up under big, black, screaming headlines. Proper people were scandalized by the *World* and called it yellow. But by 1896 some 300,000 New Yorkers a day were buying and liking it. It belonged in the urban world.

There were other ways to be amused in the city. In 1869, in Cincinnati, on a green athletic field, nine men in loose knickers, overblouses, and red stockings romped about in the game of "base ball." That in itself was not new; baseball had been around for years as a game for gentlemen amateurs. But the Cincinnati Red Stockings were a play-for-pay team to the last man. By the mid-1880s, enough people would part with a quarter or a half dollar for an "exhibition of base ball" to support two leagues and even a season's-end "world series" between the winners in the National League and those in the American Association. The more socially select might not go to baseball games, but to the theater, where they could watch Joseph Jefferson, Edwin Booth, or John Drew, best known as the uncle of a trio of stage-struck siblings whose last name was Barrymore. And of course there was the circus, under Phineas T. Barnum, that wonderful "vulgar, greasy genius," as Vernon L. Parrington called him. Barnum's show grew bigger and better annually; the wonders were touted with ever more brass and fanfare; and while the suckers who were born one to a minute dropped the money in the till, Barnum, the original public relations man, retired to a gaudy mansion on the outskirts of Bridgeport, Connecticut—no doubt to laugh himself to death. By the '90s, youngsters could watch William F. Cody, fresh from triumphs as a fighter of Indians,

re-enact those feats (with considerable gilding) in the Wild West show. What if "Buffalo Bill" took off his grease paint each night, and the red warriors who had bitten the dust got up to die again at the next matinee? The audiences did not reflect on the

BILL'S WILD WEST
ROUGH RIDERS OF THE WORLD.

COL. W. F. CODY
"BUFFALO BILL"
WILL APPEAR
AT EVERY PERFORMANCE

VBOYS, THE REAL ROUGH RIDERS OF THE WORLD WHOSE DARING EXPLOITS HAVE MADE THEIR VERY NAMES SYNONYMOUS WITH DEEDS OF BRAVERY.

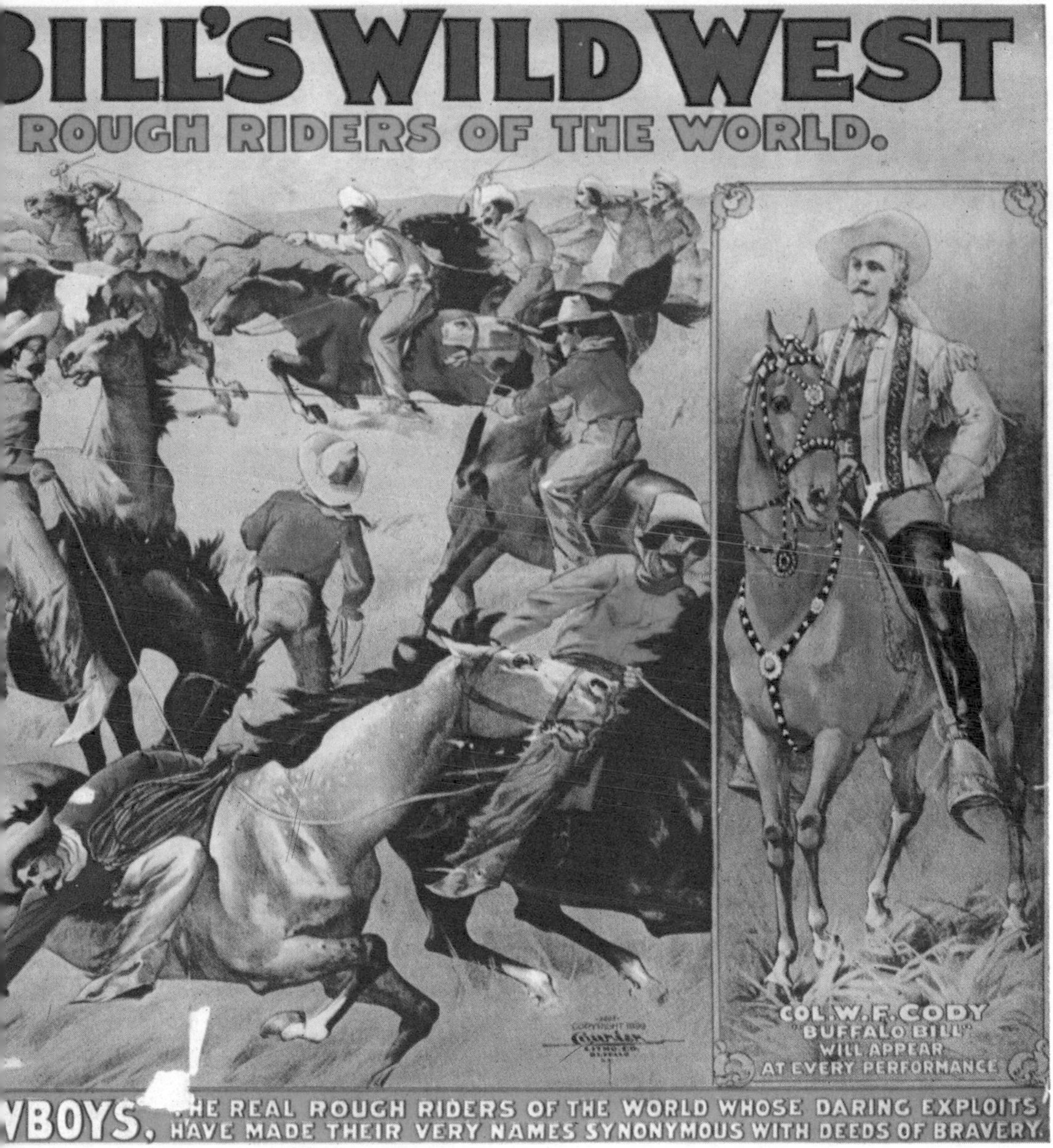

implications of the fact that Americans were changing from a nation of performers to a nation of watchers. Big-time, professional entertainment was part of the new order everywhere. For that matter, a mass revival led by Dwight L. Moody and Ira D. San-key was also something of a show.

With such attractions around, the idle youth of the cities had no lack of prospects for loafing and inviting its soul. The nation, however, was grimly determined to educate it. Between 1870 and 1910, the number of public

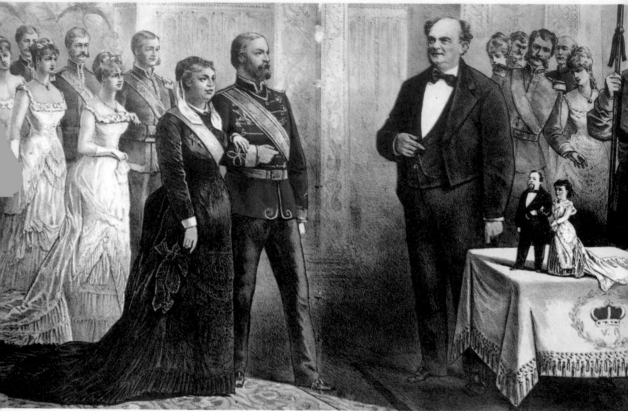

Here Lavinia and Tom Thumb are presented by P. T. Barnum to the British court of Victoria and Albert. (Actually, the midgets were twice that size.)

high schools increased from 500 to more than 10,000, and again, in the cities, the great bulk of the youthful population attended as a matter of course. The enrollment in public elementary and high schools in this period grew from 6,000,000 to more than 17,000,000, and the average number of days in the school year from 132 to 157. Also, a steadily increasing proportion of the schoolteachers were women. Thus one more opportunity was open in the cities for the independent young female. Fortunately, it was no longer necessary to establish class discipline by thrashing the oldest boy, as had been the case in the little rural schoolhouse.

The cities, too, were generally the homes of the new universities (and old colleges transforming themselves into universities) of the period from 1870 to 1900. Johns Hopkins, founded in Baltimore in 1876, and the University of Chicago, founded in 1892, were the best known of the newer ones. But in Cambridge, New York, and New Haven, Harvard, Columbia, and Yale drew upon the resources of urban wealth and leisure as they set up graduate schools, libraries, laboratories, and extension divisions. Few city dwellers knew that the modern sciences and social sciences were being born in their vicinity—that out of the laboratories and seminars where physics, biology, chemistry, sociology, economics, and jurisprudence were being taught would come ideas to transform their lives. The revolution on the campus was unheralded but real. General courses in "natural philosophy" and "the classics," conducted by rote and recitation, gave way to disciplined inquiry in specialized sub-branches of knowledge. Such developments could not have taken place outside a setting that brought together books, paintings, statuary, equipment—and courts and hospitals and churches, too—and people. In sum, an urban setting. The modern university was not, perhaps, the child of the city, but of the same centripetal forces that were making it.

The embattled uplifters

The city had its darker side as well. Growing commercial and factory districts blighted the areas around them with smoke and noise, and drove those residents who could afford it to move to the then-youthful suburbs (once the steam and electric railways put them within convenient reach). The abandoned homes were taken over, subdivided, and rented to workers' families who lived on pittances,

under the constant threat of job loss in bad times. In New York, the tenement, or multiple dwelling, was a sordid and impressive fact as early as 1890. It was searingly exposed in that year by a *Sun* reporter, Jacob Riis, in his book *How the Other Half Lives.* He painted unforgettable pictures of three- to six-story buildings crowded against one another in an airless, sunless huddle. They were often crammed with four families to a floor (though originally built for a half or a quarter of that number, or less), and these 12 or more families—60 or more people—might share one stopped-up toilet, or a single water tap. Cleanliness was impossible. Consumptive children coughed out their lives in living rooms where parents bent over piecework from sweatshops; vermin ran everywhere; fires, once started, raced through such buildings swiftly, taking a fearful toll. A New York City commission found thousands of these dwellings existing in 1894; a federal investigating body listed Baltimore's slum population in the same year at about 25,000, Philadelphia's at 35,000, and Chicago's at 162,000.

Often, though not inevitably, the slum districts had a high percentage of immigrants. Although some of the hundreds of thousands pouring into the country went out to farms in Kansas, Nebraska, or Minnesota, many more chose or were forced to accept industrial jobs. This meant urban living, and as the newcomer was often unskilled and at the bottom of the pay

The slum conditions that George Bellows saw and painted in New York (left) were not unlike those that Jane Addams (above) set out to ameliorate when she founded Hull House in Chicago in 1889.

scale, the little Italys, Bohemias, Polands, and Greeces of Boston, Chicago, and New York were often slum areas. Unthinking old-stock Americans often blamed poverty on the immigrants, particularly the recent ones from southern and eastern Europe. But the Croatian or Syrian worker who crouched in a tenement living room surrounded by his family of six or 10 was usually a victim, not a cause, of the squalor around him.

At any rate, many slum dwellers sought escape from their miseries in drink or crime or prostitution—although there were always a few who escaped through the door of luck, talent, and hard work into the more successful classes. To bring hope to those left behind was a challenge to American humanitarianism. The challenge was especially demanding to a young Midwestern girl, Jane Addams, who in 1889 opened at Hull House in Chicago the first "settlement house" —a neighborhood center for adult education, recreation, training, employment counseling, and whatever else came to hand—from scrubbing lice out of children's hair to battling the police in an effort to get them to stop demanding graft from pushcart peddlers. Presently, other women were following the gentle Jane's lead, and the middle-class "new woman" had yet another opportunity to assert her independence. She could enter the world of business, she could teach, or she could do what was called social work. In the city, at least, the walls of kitchen and nursery, behind which women were supposed to stay, were crumbling.

So the settlement worker pushed her way into the slum, which stank and was an eyesore but which also pulsed with people, noises, smells, street cries, and multilingual disputes —the slum which was crowded with life. And while she did so, other determined women revived causes born in the preurban days of the 1840s and 1850s. The year 1879 saw the formation of the Women's Christian Temperance Union. Frances Willard led hosts of wives and mothers in praying crusades before saloons, which drove

sheepish men to look elsewhere for their beer. One of the W.C.T.U.'s most notable recruits was Carrie Nation, who forsook prayer for action and became a national figure as she smashed bar furnishings with her hatchet. The other most notable convert of the women's temperance movement was the wife of President Rutherford B. Hayes, who from 1877 to 1881 ran the White House on a dry basis. Public officials at state functions privately mourned for the days of yore as they sipped the punches prepared by "Lemonade Lucy." But it could not be denied that she was a forceful woman and an example to others. Likewise, in 1869, the National Woman Suffrage Association was formed, to do for womankind what the abolitionists had done for the slave. Under Elizabeth Cady Stanton and other resolute and forceful ladies, it went on to victory with the adoption of the Nineteenth Amendment some 50 years later. (The timetable ran a bit behind that of abolitionism.)

The uplifters and reformers, too, had transferred their efforts to the city. Organization, office work, publication, and conference replaced mere moral exhortation. The signs everywhere pointed to cohesion, concentration, and method as the highroads to victory. And nowhere were these forces so well exemplified as in the city—mighty, gaudy Babylon, wicked but rich; glittering and powerful; home of the big battalions.

NEW-YORK HISTORICAL SOCIETY

THE VICTORIAN LOOK

What we call Victorian owes little to Queen Victoria, a good deal to her consort Prince Albert, and most of all to the Industrial Revolution. That revolution made it possible to mass-produce furniture and similar items that previously had been handcrafted and therefore available only to the wealthy. It also produced a new, prosperous middle class, but one unsure of its taste. The manufacturers did little to help; English industrial design was at a low ebb. Prince Albert's special contribution was the great Crystal Palace exhibition of 1851. This rich display of arts, crafts, and machinery from all over the world opened English eyes and whetted English appetites. Actually, the comfortable middle-class home had been on its way even before Victoria came to the throne in 1837. The one above is typical late Victorian, with the gladiator on the mantel clock, the wicker rocker, and even the Newfoundland dog, which no previous generation had seen any reason to bring into the house.

948

THE MACHINE AGE ENTERS THE PARLOR

This family group painted by Frederick Spencer in 1840 shows clearly the effect of the Industrial Revolution on the home. The carpet is a product of the Jacquard loom, invented in 1801. Formerly, only the rich had woven rugs; people who could not afford them had hooked or rag rugs or nothing. Marble had been the material of palaces. Now, thanks to the steam engine, it could be quarried mechanically, and the marble-topped table became one of the new status symbols. On the negative side, the graceless design of the sofa, footstool, and table are clearly dictated by the limitations of the machine.

THE VICTORIAN LOOK

FROM RICH TO ORNATE

As Victorianism progressed, it became more and more fancifully fussy. A passion for draping any object or surface developed (above), and furniture became more deeply padded and tufted (right). The vase (left) was displayed in the Philadelphia Centennial Exhibition of 1876, which awakened American interest in the decorative arts in much the same way the Crystal Palace exhibition had done in England.

THE VICTORIAN LOOK

FROM ORNATE TO EXOTIC

To create the "exotic" and the "picturesque" were avowed decorating aims of the day, and of all the influences to this end, none was more popular than the Moorish. It might be handled conservatively, as in the John D. Rockefeller sitting room at the left, or it might be used inappropriately for objects like the sewing machine at the right. In the late 1800s, it came to a magnificent, dust-collecting maturity with the "Turkish cozy corner" (above).

COLLECTION OF LESLIE DORSEY

GODEY'S "AMERICANISED" PARIS FASHIONS.

GODEY'S FASHIONS FOR MARCH 1870

THE VICTORIAN LOOK

THE WELL-DRAPED WOMAN

The Victorian lady of the house had two bibles in addition to the King James version. One was the work of an English architect named Charles Eastlake. Titled *Hints on Household Taste,* it appeared in 1872 and told the lady what to put in her home. The second was *Godey's Lady's Book,* which told her what to wear (left and above) and set the style for many more women than its 150,000 circulation seemed to indicate. The mid-Victorian female was as heavily petticoated and gowned as her rooms were draped, but as the century drew to a close, a trend to lighter, easier dress and furniture emerged.

OVERLEAF: Mid-Victorian elegance permeates this painting of the Hatch family of New York by Eastman Johnson, who asked and got $1,000 a head. The double curtains are to protect the room from the housewife's dread enemy—sunlight, which faded the colors of her furnishings.

956

MACHINE-AGE CULTURE

Late in 1877, workmen built in Cambridge, Massachusetts, a three-story mansard-roofed house for a huge, bearded philosopher-historian-writer-lecturer named John Fiske. It was a big house for a man important to his time. In a long career that began as an undergraduate at Harvard in the '60s and ended with death in 1901, Fiske enthralled millions with the belief that America was the finest end product of evolution. He began as a disciple of the Englishman Herbert Spencer, who was responsible for applying the doctrines of Darwin to all fields of human study. Darwin's biology taught that nature was constantly creating new species of plant and animal life at random; that some were suited to their environment and lived, while others suffered extinction. Spencer compressed this into the catch phrase "survival of the fittest," and went on to explain, in a multitude of volumes, that human institutions— religions, languages, societies, nations —were also "organisms" (like plants,

The Columbian Exposition was meant to show the progress that the human race, particularly in the United States, had made.

animals, and humans) and went through the same cycles of growth and change and adaptation. One single principle doomed Carthage and the three-toed sloth, but sent the giraffe and the British Parliament marching triumphantly into the 19th century.

Fiske, in 1874, had given Spencer a New England American stamp in his book *Outlines of Cosmic Philosophy.* Evolution came through, but more clearly under God's direction, and more clearly moving "upward" to "better" things. Where biology simply said "change," Fiske said "improvement." And in the final quarter of the 19th century, he wrote a series of histories of the United States that were balm to the self-esteem of a fast-growing country. The great principles of individual liberty and organization, according to Fiske, were developed and reconciled in the tribal councils of the Teutonic peoples who dwelt unconquered in the forests of northern Europe during the Roman Empire's heyday. Descendants of these same peoples brought the sparks of self-rule to the British Isles. A small handful of Puritans carried these "Anglo-

Andrew Carnegie championed one type of Social Darwinism—the "gospel of wealth"—insisting the rich (and thus the "fittest") must help their fellow men.

Saxon" gifts to the New World to protect them from a wicked king in 1630. And in 1776 the American people, in proclaiming their independence, preserved the civilizing forces of freedom and order against another mistaken monarch. The Constitution of 1787 struck the perfect and ideal balance between the two mighty forces, and the progress of the United States was evidence that the Founding Fathers had ridden the wave of the future. The English-speaking peoples, under representative governments, had survived and prospered, and clearly they were the "fittest." The best findings of modern science, Fiske maintained, seemed only to demonstrate what Americans had suspected all along—that they were chosen among nations to excel—a theme that runs from the writings of the Puritan founders of New England to the *Gettysburg Address.* It was no wonder that Fiske sold extraordinarily well for a historian—and lived well on the proceeds.

The view advanced by Fiske came to be known as Social Darwinism,

960

which was simply the idea that existing institutions had weathered the challenge of the environment and were therefore chosen by nature herself for perpetuation. It was a lovely justification of the *status quo,* a perfect warrant for smugness. It could be used to defend a bit of overseas land grabbing, as it was by a Congregational clergyman, Josiah Strong. He wrote, in 1885, that a "marked characteristic of the Anglo-Saxon is what may be called an instinct or genius for colonizing," and that "this powerful race" would move out from its American base "down upon Mexico, down upon Central and South America, out upon the islands of the sea, over upon Africa and beyond." Could anyone doubt, Strong asked, that the result would be the survival of the fittest? Or Social Darwinism could be used as a club against any policy of government assistance to the powerless, as it was by Yale sociologist William Graham Sumner. Nature, he noted, "grants her rewards to the fittest . . . without regard to other considerations of any kind. If we do not like it, and if we try to amend it, there is only one way in which we can do it. We can take from the better and give to the worse." In other words, "We shall favor the survival of the unfittest, and we shall accomplish this by destroying liberty." For liberty meant, eventually, "inequality." And how could individuals down on their luck redeem themselves from this iron law? By "an enhancement of the industrial virtues

Booker T. Washington, born a slave, became a great black leader despite some beliefs that most of his people reject today.

and of the moral forces which thence arise. Industry, self-denial, and temperance are the laws of prosperity for men and states."

If this rather grim view of the possibilities of social change found solid lodgment in some universities, it must be added that the same universities were already training men like William James, Edward A. Ross, Richard T. Ely, and John Dewey, who would react against it. But Social Darwinism did lend the sanction of intellectuals to the new American order of millionaires and laborers, big cities and big spending—an order uncongenial to the old idea of America as a kind of Roman republic of hardy, virtuous landowners. That was the rub, in fact. America seemed to be moving in the direction of ancient Rome, from simplicity to imperial wallowing in fleshpots. Social Darwinism said this was not the case; bigness was best, and ordained. And one particular offshoot of Social Darwinism proved especially useful in the '90s, when protests against big business picked up in volume. This was known as the "gospel of wealth."

Its most popular spokesman was Andrew Carnegie. When he published the article *The Gospel of Wealth* in *The North American Review* in 1889, readers sat up and took note, for the steelmaster knew wealth firsthand. Carnegie was always a genial millionaire, frankly enjoying his money, and rather liking his self-chosen role of businessman-intellectual, explaining to the world why the rich apparently got richer and what they should do about it. He was well fitted for the mission, because, unlike some of his fellow tycoons, he read and understood books. In his article, he repeated the Darwinian notion that the financially fattest were the fittest, but insisted that this was all the more reason for them to use their gains wisely. They should distribute their riches among worthy causes, shun ostentation, and above all refrain from showering wealth on their dependents. Thus, in

the next generation, the truly virtuous would be enabled to rise to their proper stations. The rich, in short, should assist in the process of natural selection to which they themselves owed their wealth. They were the trustees for evolution. Once again, this played old tunes on new instruments. Churches had been teaching for a long time that the rich were only stewards of their treasures. The title deeds were vested in the Lord.

The new gospel was a moral justification for the accumulation of wealth as an end in life. Late 19th-century listeners were told that the search for it was an honorable and laudable ambition. Those already on financial pinnacles called down encouragingly: Money is power, and there is nothing wrong with power as long as it is used for worthy purposes. Prophets arose to spread the word. One of the best known was Russell H. Conwell, a Baptist minister who delivered his lecture *Acres of Diamonds* thousands of times to aspiring youngsters. "I say that you ought to get rich, and it is your duty to get rich," he told them. "To make money honestly is to preach the gospel." And money, or even the love of it, was not the root of all evil. "In the hands of good men and women it could accomplish, and it has accomplished, good." What was more, chances to get rich were always at hand. The title of the lecture came from the story of a man who had vainly hunted treasure around the world, while acres of diamonds lay

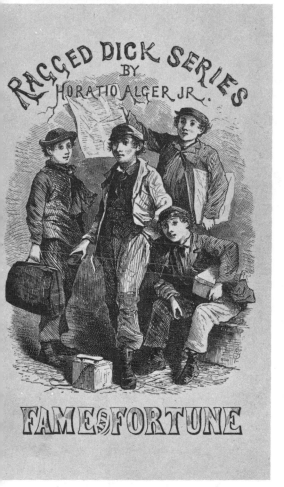

By struggling against odds and working to achieve wealth and honor, the heroes in Horatio Alger's books represented the ideal for the American boy.

buried, unknown to him, in his own back yard.

Conwell was only expressing formally the idea that ran through the dozens of novels published by Horatio Alger, beginning in 1867. In them, poor boys were always given one lucky break, and then by their virtue and sobriety, they made themselves success models. "He was no longer Ragged Dick now, but Mr. Richard Hunter, junior partner in the large firm of Rockwell & Hunter . . . . So Dick has achieved FAME AND FORTUNE." And in 1895, Booker T. Washington, in an address at Atlanta, told fellow Southern blacks to "cast down your bucket where you are." If the black man would forgo the dream of acquiring political equality and the white man's cultural luxuries, and would keep clean, toil,

Mark Twain's contriving Tom Sawyer persuades a friend to take over the uninspiring job of whitewashing a fence and wisely observes that "In order to make a . . . boy covet a thing, it is only necessary to make the thing difficult to attain."

and save diligently, progress simply could not be denied him. (Washington himself was, in his own eyes, a living example—from slave boy to guest at the White House, through hard work.) Thus was the old New England gospel of frugality and labor as the sign of salvation modernized. It was hawked over the book counters in Alger's works, proclaimed from the pulpit by Conwell, decked in new terminology by Carnegie, and offered as the cure to the race problem by a black man, Washington, who had learned his lessons well, in reconstruction days, from a New England schoolteacher settled in the South.

Literary giants and pygmies

The leading magazines of the upper-middle and upper classes in the '80s and '90s were showcases of a changing literature. *Harper's Monthly Magazine, The Century, The Atlantic Monthly, Lippincott's* and others carried the work of Mark Twain, William Dean Howells, Bret Harte, Sarah Orne Jewett, George Washington Cable, Joel Chandler Harris, as well as other writers now largely forgotten. Literary generalizations are perilous, but the dominating force of the period among the first-class writers seemed to be, for want of a better word, realism—though something needs to be said about a few lesser fry who deliberately blurred reality with consequences that are still felt. The good writers of this period were trying, like their literary predecessors—Emerson, Whitman, Hawthorne, Cooper, Irving—to find out what was unique in the American experience. They were probing for the particular commitments and opportunities of American life, just when it was in the most violent kind of flux. But, unlike the romantics who came before them, they dealt less with ideals and abstractions than with the concrete and immediate experiences of living. Nobody knew or cared what Hester Prynne ate for breakfast, but readers were told exactly what Huckleberry Finn loaded in his canoe when he escaped from his father's clutches. That was part of the difference between Hawthorne and Mark Twain. Yet *The Scarlet Letter* and *Huckleberry Finn* were both novels about people who violated the codes of their respective societies. It was not the problems of the new literature that were different; it was the methods.

By common consent, Henry James, Mark Twain, and Howells were the three greatest novelists to emerge in the years from 1865 to 1900. James, spending most of his life abroad, dealt with the interaction of Europeans and Americans in works of extraordinary sensibility and intricately convoluted style. His characters were people of means who scarcely knew there was such a thing as a factory, a plow, a gun, or a butcher's bill. He had, therefore, little in common with that American writer whom Emerson had sought—the one who would sing "the meal in the firkin, the milk in the pan." His place is in a world of his own, which has its rewards, but from which many are barred if they long for something robust after a long diet of refined intellectuality.

Mark Twain was, in the words of his friend Howells, "the Lincoln of our literature." His most productive years came when he had settled down to a home and respectability in Hartford, Connecticut. Born Samuel L. Clemens in 1835, he had been a river pilot, silver miner, and newspaperman before he broke fully into the public eye with *Innocents Abroad* in 1869. This was an account of a voyage to Europe and the Holy Land, in which the "barbarian" from the "Wild West" uproariously pokes fun at Europe's artistic shrines and the tourist suckers who come to gawk at them. But what is significant is that Twain voluntarily went back to Europe many times, enjoying the experience, and milking more books from it on each occasion. He was the conscientious bourgeois admiring the cathedral, and the urchin throwing a snowball at the tourist's top hat. This polarity—this yearning for what was fresh and unspoiled, and at the same time for the success that cloyed it—was the mark of his life, and of his writings. Twain smoked, drank, cussed, and played the bad boy; yet he married and adored a respectable businessman's daughter from Elmira, New York, and was a model Hartford citizen, striving to get rich not only by his writings but by investing in inventions, publishing houses, and other properties that never, somehow, paid off. He caricatured the love of gimmicks in Tom Sawyer, who forever seeks a gaudy and complicated way to do a simple thing; yet he himself was always eager to be the first in town to put a new

Max Beerbohm's drawing Walt Whitman Inciting the Bird of Freedom To Soar *is meant to be both comic and critical.*

gadget, whether a typewriter or a telephone, in his home. In *Huckleberry Finn* (1884), Huck drifts idyllically down the Mississippi on the raft with Jim, the runaway slave. These are two unspoiled human beings, both children in one sense and adult in another. They are free to develop a relationship to each other outside the master-slave code of the South, and free to see through the pretensions of the people they meet along the river. (The King and the Duke are prime examples.) But in the end, Jim is captured, and Tom Sawyer appears to direct the rescue operation. The attempt fails, ruined by idiocies derived from Tom's garbled reading. Tom, however, is satisfied; he has had his hour upon the stage. But because the 1880s demanded at least something happy in every ending, it turns out that Jim was already free by the terms of his owner's will. And Huck? His only happiness is in escape; he is going to "light out for the territory." Unfortunately, neither Mark Twain nor America could light out for the territory by 1890. And so Twain continued to write books that created laughter, and privately to pour out his bitterness against the damned human race. Toward the end of his days he was lionized, lauded, publicized, and courted as much as any man could wish, but the river towns of his boyhood had sunk forever in the mists of the past. He had to be a grown man in a grown America, to face life as it was and not as it was imagined. It was asking him to drink a poisoned cup.

Howells never equaled Twain's power, but his output was prodigious. He had been born in a small Ohio town in 1837, and lived ripely on into the 20th century. His novels are distinguished by the faithful detail in which he depicted the lives of the middle classes—in shop, office, kitchen, vacation hotel, newspaper editorial room, dinner party, and literally hundreds of other situations. He was aware of the temptations of maturity. In *The Rise of Silas Lapham,* a good and sweet Vermont businessman is plunged into a sea of troubles when his paint company becomes enormously successful. His problems in finding the right matches for his daughters and in defining some comfortable existence for himself outside of his work are deftly drawn. He meets a series of business misfortunes, is given the chance to get out of them by a deal that borders on dishonesty, and saves himself by refusing. In the end he is back where he started, in the countryside, with his fortune gone but his self-respect intact. If this was not quite the ending for many similar stories in the America of Grant and Garfield, Howells could not be accused of being a Pollyanna nonetheless. In *A Modern Instance*, Bartley Hubbard, a sharp New England youth, becomes a city journalist, and (possibly as a result!) slides unchecked into moral decay. Yet in the novels of Howells, human beings remain the makers of moral choices, even the

Mark Twain is caricatured as a Southern writer, lounging in a hammock with a mint julep nearby and a corncob pipe in hand.

wrong ones. By the end of the century, a new school of realism was insisting that humans were perhaps the pawns of overwhelming natural forces. Stephen Crane's *Maggie: A Girl of the Streets*, in 1892, suggested that Maggie had no choice but "vice" open to her by the very circumstances of her upbringing. And in 1901, Frank Norris' *The Octopus*, a fictionized tale of the Southern Pacific Railroad and its war with California farmers, made the railroad barons and the shippers alike victims rather than

George Washington Cable was the leading "local-color" interpreter
New England after 1885 because of antisegregation views, he w

South, starting with Old Creole Days *in 1879. A resident of writing of his homeland in 1914, as this poster shows.*

agents of the same elemental power that grew the wheat itself.

Twain and Howells, by 1900, were both unhappy with what America had become. Howells still had hope of a transformation of American industrialism that would replace class warfare and brutal exploitation with Christian socialism. Twain saw no such hope of making American equality live again; his final judgment was anger at all classes—and at himself—for the crime of being human. Walt Whitman is generally spoken of as a literary figure of the postwar period, although the first edition of *Leaves of Grass* appeared in 1855. Whitman's unashamed paeans to the common man, democracy, the American land, the infinite beauty of things themselves—from carpenters' tools to steam locomotives—make him an important spokesman for the hustling mood of the Gilded Age. Because he spoke frankly of the body electric, and spat good-naturedly upon the rules of prosody required of "genteel" poets in his age, he is one of the forerunners of the uninhibited in modern American literature. What he tried to say with his catalogues was that out of the common, something beautiful might arise; out of materialism, something beyond the material—in America, at any rate. He was a true poet of 19th-century American democracy, with its faults and hopes alike.

The so-called "local-color school" represented another kind of realism. Sarah Orne Jewett, for example, in *The Country of the Pointed Firs* sketches New Englanders who are solidly rooted in their little worlds—real, dignified, individually painted by a thousand details of dress, speech, and manner, carefully re-created. New England's greatness may be gone, but these, her people, remain. George Washington Cable, in such works as *Old Creole Days*, rendered the same service for the old French-speaking families of Louisiana. There is the smell of sea and river in these stories, and strong hints of the sadness of life and the varying sturdinesses and weaknesses with which it can be met. (Cable, though a Southerner to his bones, was driven to live in Massachusetts after 1885 because he openly condemned segregation.)

To set against the work of these local colorists, there was a certain amount of pseudo "regionalism." The Western stories of Bret Harte are examples. Their gamblers with hearts of gold, or miners who become Argonauts, or gold seekers, without being tainted by greed, are pure frauds. Likewise, the mid-1880s saw the publication, in the *Century* magazine, of several stories by Thomas Nelson Page, later collected in a volume, *In Ole Virginia*. In such tales as *Marse Chan* and *Meh Lady*, Page dipped his pen in magnolia juice and drew an "Old South" of "darkies" laughing in soft contentment, girls of marble beauty, and prideful young planter-aristocrats whose blood was properly hot on the battlefield and cool in the

Winslow Homer was realistically portraying his world of art when he painted himself and two friends as they sketched the cloud patterns over the mountains.

drawing room. The South of Page had nothing to do with the real South, of penniless Scotchmen and Irishmen who had quarreled and brawled their way across a virgin Southwest and made it a cotton kingdom and themselves its nobles; or the South of middle-size farmers who worked hard at their crops, never owned a slave, hunted and fished when they could, sucked the jug, jigged to the fiddle, and got saved at revival meetings. Or, for that matter, the South of slavery as it was, with its muted savagery on both sides, as well as its sporadic kindness. But Page's South, unfortunately, became real in the eyes of a whole generation of Northerners and Southerners alike. And in the same way, when Owen Wister wrote *The Virginian* (1902), he created an impossible cowboy hero—one of nature's noblemen, who can kill his enemy without facing the moral ambiguities or consequences of his act; who admits no emotion the privilege of being spoken; and who solves most of his problems by riding off into the sagebrush. In the novel, this wooden paragon marries an Eastern schoolteacher; one

971

Max Schmitt was painted by Thomas Eakins—with a flesh-and-bone truthfulness, as in his portraits—on the Schuylkill River in Philadelphia in 1871.

wonders what they said to each other after the honeymoon.

Yet the creators of false local color were, in a sense, also products of the era. As the genuine artists in regionalism were trying to fix the lines of a vanishing variety of folkways, so the purveyors of a nonexistent West and South were creating shadow shows that distracted men from considering the genuine human consequences (good and bad alike) of the oncoming industrial order.

Dozens of other writers, great and small, contributed to the national letters in the century's last 20 years. Many are worth note; others wrote ephemera; all in some ways reflected the breath-taking facts of sudden change. Between 1840 and 1890, men were hurled from the age of riverboat and pack mule into that of electricity, the railroad, the trust, even the skyscraper. All things were made new. The relationships between individuals and classes, always somewhat complicated by a lack of tradition and by the pressures of democracy in America, had to be worked out freshly again. Small wonder literature presented not one but many aspects.

Canvas, brick, and mortar

Artists in America, before the Civil War, had tended to imitate classical and romantic models supplied by Europe. Perhaps because of the self-confidence of the postwar era, perhaps for other reasons, young painters turned to native subjects after 1865. Many of them, moreover, handled their materials with the same attention to the workaday reality that we have seen in Howells and other novelists. Among these were artists like Thomas Eakins, Winslow Homer, and Albert Pinkham Ryder. Homer gained much of his experience during the war as field illustrator for *Harper's Weekly*. Later, his portrayal of the New England seacoast had enormous appeal; such work as his belongs with writings like those of Mary Wilkins Freeman and Sarah Orne Jewett.

Eakins delved deeply into studies of anatomy to perfect his figures, the results of which are shown in works like *The Swimming Hole*. His insistence on anatomical knowledge as the first step in art got him into hot water. While a teacher at the Pennsylvania Academy, he asked female students to sketch men in the nude. Victorian propriety would not stand for this, and he was discharged. All his portraits have a flesh-and-bone truthfulness about them. They said, in an age given to posturing and denying its workaday origins, "This is how real men and women look, every day, and they are interesting." As for Ryder, he was a specialist in striking effects of depth and density; his paintings are full of mysterious and haunting images that suggest something unsuspected lurking behind the reality we see.

Artists in bronze and marble produced many memorable works in the postwar period; Augustus Saint-Gaudens' statues of General Sherman in New York and of Lincoln in Chicago show that the Civil War had considerable effect on the monumental arts in America. And Daniel Chester French's *Minute Man*, at Concord, Massachusetts, is another well-known moment of history in bronze. French also did the Lincoln seated with his hands on the arms of the chair, thoughtfully staring at the crowds who lift their faces to him in the Lincoln Memorial in Washington.

Art and engineering combined, in the '80s and '90s, to produce a new kind of architecture. The development of the electric elevator and cheap steel made higher buildings possible. When having offices 10 or more stories above the street presented no problems, and when walls hung on a steel frame bore no weight, and thus did not need to be thickened at the base for each added foot of height, the sky was almost literally the limit. The first skyscraper, according to many authorities, was the Home Insurance Building in Chicago, designed by William L. Jenney and completed in 1885. Other architects like Daniel Burnham, John Root, and Louis Sullivan struck out boldly to design

OVERLEAF: *The Transportation Building at the Columbian Exposition was designed by Louis Sullivan, now considered the father of modern architecture. His belief that the outward form of a building should express the function beneath is basic to modern architecture throughout the world.*

975

buildings that would express the possibilities of the new age. Sullivan in particular combined massive structures with intricate external detail; his Auditorium Building in Chicago is one of his best and best-known works. What he hoped to do was to create a functional architecture, which would express the spirit of the activities carried on inside each building. His buildings, and others of this early skyscraper era, give a sense of the power of the city, the creativity of the urban hive, and yet the potentialities for order, proportion, and harmony even in great public structures. Sul-livan's most famous pupil and disciple, and a lifelong admirer, was Frank Lloyd Wright.

Whether it is called the Gilded Age or the Brown Decades or Victorian America, the 30-year period that ended the 19th century was the corridor from an earlier, simpler America to the one we know today. It was a time when materialism and science flowered, when technological and physical expansion dizzied men by their incredible pace, when problems multiplied so quickly that the institutions meant to handle them buckled under the strain. In religion, journal-

The Octagon Room of the Waldorf Hotel at 34th Street and Fifth Avenue is the setting for this millinery poster of 1893.

ism, art, letters, architecture, manners—everywhere this sign of sudden expansion was evident. Such expansion led to ostentation without and questionings within. Inside American life, as the '90s wore on, social conflicts seethed. Great strikes rocked the nation, and the farmers raised the countryside in revolt. Yet the higher the inner fires burned, the more unrestrained became the worship of money and the display of what it could buy. And perhaps this was because Americans felt their wealth was not merely an accident, but something that, in a sense, they had earned. If it confused them, they were nonetheless proud of it.

For America's gay Gilded Age reflected not only the nation's seeming triumph over poverty and early material deficiencies. It also advertised to the world a kind of victory for what long had been called "the democratic experiment." It *seemed* to say that man, if left unfettered by governmental, traditional, or historic restrictions, could turn the wilderness into an economic Garden of Eden where there was plenty for all and want for none. It *appeared* to be the triumph of *laissez faire* and the final vindication of the theory of democracy. As Americans stood back and looked at what they had wrought, they could not help finding it good.

They were a success. And if success was measured in dollars and cents—why, that was not unnatural. In the race for riches, a lack of social origins did not handicap an enterprising man. The game was open to all. Opportunity beckoned everywhere for the persistent, and around every corner lay the promised land. Or so men thought. In such a bonanza mood, it was understandable that gain was foremost in the popular mind. And if some of the achievements of the nation were only gilt, and not pure gold—why, that was understandable, too.

MAIN TEXT CONTINUES IN VOLUME 12

Mrs. Gardner and Her Palace

A SPECIAL CONTRIBUTION BY
NELSON LANSDALE

Ever an individualist, "Mrs. Jack" startled proper Bostonians when she built an Italian palace in the "Athens of America", filled it with art for the public later to enjoy.

Venetian lions guard the entrance, a doorway imported from Florence, to the Isabella Stewart Gardner Museum in Boston. Above the door is emblazoned the owner's defiant motto: *C'est mon plaisir.* Pleasure has never been quite respectable in Boston, but neither in her prime was the flamboyant Mrs. Jack, with her Paris gowns and carriages, her spectacular jewels and flowers, her retinue of writers, painters, musicians, and actors.

Henry James called Mrs. Gardner's a "preposterously pleasant career," and the memory of it stays green at Fenway Court, the elaborate Italian palace she designed and built near the Boston Museum of Fine Arts, and which, as her will directed, remains almost exactly as she left it forever in 1924. Nothing may be added to, subtracted from, or importantly altered at Fenway Court, which was also her home for 21 years. As a museum, it is not much in the news because it is as static as the pyramids (in the shadow of which, one

Fenway Court, built in 1902 as Mrs. Gardner's residence, was planned as an eventual museum. The galleries open off the courtyard with its Venetian arches and a Roman mosaic pavement.

moonlight night, Isabella once brooded so much on Cleopatra that she completely forgot it was Christmas Eve).

The daughter of a wealthy New York merchant, Belle Stewart became a member of one of Boston's first families through her marriage to John L. Gardner. Never quite a lady within the strict Boston meaning of the word, she had a temper with which Khrushchev's might seem pale by comparison, a sense of showmanship from which P. T. Barnum might have taken lessons. She loved old masters, young men, and music. With their help, she took Boston by storm.

Surveying American collections, the authoritative *Art News* ranked the Gardner fourth in America, after the Metropolitan and the Frick in New York and the National Gallery in Washington. Although it owns fewer than 60 Italian old masters, Philip Hendy (later Sir Philip and director of London's National Gallery) in 1931 ranked it fifth in the world in this field, following only the Uffizi Gallery in Florence, the Kaiser Friedrich Museum in Berlin, the National Gallery in London, and the Louvre. Even now, when the National Gallery in Washington is added to this list, the Gardner ranks sixth. Located across the Charles River only a mile or two from Harvard's Fogg Museum of Art, where the vast majority of American museum curators and directors have been trained, the Gardner collection has served as an additional laboratory for their studies. Thus Fenway Court has had an important influence on the molding of taste in America.

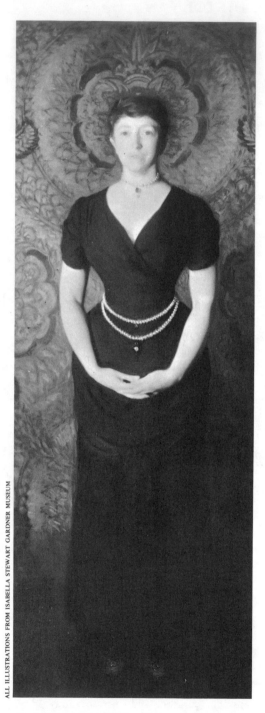

Mrs. Gardner had John Singer Sargent recognize her love of pearls by painting her in 1888 with more strings of them than she then owned.

In buying old masters, Mrs. Gardner was a generation ahead of tycoons like Andrew Mellon and Henry Clay Frick. The latter's collection, housed in the sumptuous Fifth Avenue mansion that was briefly his home, most nearly in America resembles her own. And if she did not always get what she thought she was buying (and who does?)—a Filippo Lippi that turned out to be a Pesellino, a Clouet now ascribed to Corneille de Lyon, and supposed works by Correggio, Tintoretto, and Bronzino now attributed to followers of those painters—she could always point to verification of her treasures by the man who until his death in 1959 was the world's leading authority on Italian Renaissance art. This was her protege Bernard Berenson, the brilliant Lithuanian-born youngster from Harvard whose studies in Europe she helped finance.

One of the first lion hunters in American society, Belle knew everybody worth knowing. If photographic evidence and her portraits by Sargent, Whistler, and Anders Zorn may be believed, she was extremely plain of face. But a long list of the most brilliant men of her time paid her homage while her adoring, well-bred husband paid her bills. As Oliver Wendell Holmes put it, "Mr. Gardner has wealth and position; Miss Stewart has wealth and charm. The alliance must be satisfactory to both families." (It was not.)

The climax of her career as collector and hostess, her most shining hour, was the opening of Fenway Court on New Year's night, 1903. She had bought the barren, swampy wasteland on which it stood in 1899, and if no woman of her time had a more lively flair for publicity, Mrs. Gardner could be as discreet as Plymouth Rock when she wanted to keep a secret. Speculation mounted as her Renaissance palace took shape, but Belle gave no interviews, dispensed no information. Although she showed a few foreign friends like actress Ellen Terry, tragedian Henry Irving, and the Archbishop of Canterbury through the house before the opening, she wanted her big surprise to bowl Boston over. It did.

At 10:30 p.m., ablaze with her famous pearls and two huge diamonds set like the antennae of a butterfly in her hair, she stood atop a horseshoe-shaped staircase in the Music Room (afterward replaced by the Spanish Cloister). Muttering their protests but consumed with curiosity, 300 of her friends and enemies—the cream of Back Bay society—clambered up one staircase to greet their hostess and marched down the other. Fifty members of the Boston Symphony Orchestra under her friend Gericke played Bach, Mozart, Schumann, and Chausson for an hour as the suspense mounted. Finally, on cue, a mirrored door rolled back and the invited guests saw for the first time the three-storied courtyard, scented with tropical flowers, aglow with orange lanterns from Paris and thousands of candles, the fountains tinkling, nasturtiums trailing down from the eight balconies taken from the Ca d'Oro in Venice. And beyond the orchids in the palm trees waited the old masters displayed in gallery after gallery on three floors.

The opening night was exactly what Belle intended it to be—breath-taking. Mrs. Jack had finally won the Battle of Boston; she had also pioneered in the creation of a new kind of museum in America. To posterity, of course, it is the museum and not the social triumph that matters. James J. Rorimer, former director of the Metropolitan Museum and head of its medieval branch, The Cloisters, once said that Mrs. Gardner was the first person in this country to incorporate specimens of Roman, Byzantine, Romanesque, and Gothic architectural detail in a building designed to display paintings. She was "thus the predecessor of George Grey Barnard, setting the pace for the magnificent achievements of The Cloisters themselves." Diplomat and historian Henry Adams, who helped her buy the 13th-century stained-glass window in the Chapel—often called the finest in this country, and which may have come from the Abbey of St. Denis—wrote her a bread-and-butter note for the star-spangled evening: "You have given me a great pleasure and greater astonishment. . . . As long as such a work can be done, I will not despair of our age, though I do not think anyone else could have done it." A rival collector, Henry E. Huntington—who succeeded

in getting Gainsborough's *Blue Boy* for his San Marino, California, library after Mrs. Gardner had failed to buy it from Grosvenor House in London—called Fenway Court "the greatest work done by an American woman."

Mrs. Gardner began as a collector with rare books in 1874. Her acquisitions, still on view, included a 1481 Dante with plates after Botticelli, a Book of Hours that had belonged to Mary, Queen of Scots, and a holograph manuscript of *Paul Revere's Ride* by Longfellow. She put book collecting aside after 1886, when Henry James took her to

The Chigi Madonna, *one of the two Botticellis in the collection, is from his earliest period. It once hung in Prince Chigi's palace in Rome.*

The most celebrated old master at Fenway Court is The Rape of Europa, *painted by Titian for Philip II of Spain in 1562. Rubens called it "the greatest painting in the world."*

John Singer Sargent's London studio to see his famous portrait of the French actress Madame Gautreau—the *Madame X* now in the Metropolitan Museum. When they met, she was 48, he 32, impressive and handsome,

a member of the New England aristocracy who had traveled all over Europe. Belle promptly commissioned her own portrait, which she unsuccessfully tried to persuade Sargent to declare the artistic equal of the

Portrait of Madame X. (That it is not).

The guides at Fenway Court now pause before the portrait in the most conspicuous spot in the Gothic Room, which Sargent used as a studio for a few months (and where Belle herself once demonstrated with a broadaxe exactly how hand-hewn her oak beams should look). The portrait was Sargent's ninth try with his restless subject; after eight failures, he was almost ready to abandon the project altogether. Mrs. Gardner insisted that nine was her mystic number, and on the ninth attempt the artist succeeded in getting a mutually satisfactory likeness. She wears a plain black dress and the famous pearls with the pendant ruby. The beauty of her bare arms caused so much comment when the picture was exhibited in Boston that her husband, who appeared to be complacent enough about the unconventional aspects of her friendship with Sargent, never again allowed the portrait to be shown, nor was the public admitted to the Gothic Room, where it hung, until after her death.

Sargent traveled with the Gardners in Italy, in France, and especially in Spain; he was their constant guest both on Beacon Street and at their summer home in Brookline. When Gardner became trustee and treasurer of the Boston Museum of Fine Arts, Sargent was commissioned to paint the entrance murals. After Gardner's death in 1898, Sargent was Mrs. Jack's constant companion when he was in America. Their romance is the subject of a 1951 novel, *The Lady and the Painter,* by the late Countess Eleanor Palffy, who maintains that their relationship was platonic. Half a century later it cannot matter much.

In Seville, in 1888, Mrs. Gardner bought her first old master—a Zurbaran Madonna. Eventually placed in the Spanish Cloister, it served as a kind of altarpiece when her body lay awaiting burial in 1924 in a room dominated by one of Sargent's undoubted early masterpieces, the swirling *El Jaleo,* a present to Mrs. Jack from Thomas Jefferson Coolidge. Maintaining that this huge dramatic picture of a dancer in a Spanish cafe had never been properly lighted when loaned to various exhibitions, Mrs. Gardner tore out the Music Room at Fenway Court to build the Spanish Cloister as a special setting for *El Jaleo.* Today, as in her lifetime, it is lighted from below to correspond to the illumination of the cafe that Sargent pictured.

Mrs. Gardner called Rembrandt's self-portrait at the age of 23 "the cornerstone of the collection" because it was the first picture she bought with public exhibition in mind. Although it was also coveted by the National Gallery in London, this painting cost Mrs. Gardner a mere $15,000, plus a fee to Berenson, who described it as "one of the most precious pictures in existence." She was less lucky with another Rembrandt she wanted, *The Old Mill,* which was eventually acquired by P. A. B. Widener of Philadelphia and now hangs in the National Gallery of Art in Washington. Berenson managed to get her the fine *Landscape with Obelisk* as a kind of consolation prize for missing out on *The Old Mill.* In Paris, a drop of her handkerchief outsmarted both the National Gallery and the Louvre when she bought Vermeer's *The Concert* for a piddling $6,000. One of some 36 works by this master, it could not have been had for 10 times that amount a decade later, and would quickly fetch far more than $1,000,000 today.

Mrs. Gardner's most celebrated old master is Titian's *The Rape of Europa.* Finished for Philip II of Spain in 1562, when Titian was past 85, it is the foremost work of his in America. Rubens, who made the copy of it, now in Madrid's Prado, called it "the greatest picture in the world." His pupil Van Dyck copied the copy; Mrs. Jack bought that, too.

And *Europa* is by no means the only Gardner picture with royal associations. Mantegna's *Holy Conversation* belonged to Charles I of England and later to Philip IV of Spain, who in turn is represented by a Velazquez portrait. Richard Norton, director of the American Academy in Rome, got the Mantegna for her, along with a Roman sarcophagus. (Countess Palffy tells of the occasion when Richard Norton's famous father, Harvard professor Charles Eliot Norton, was ushered by mistake into the glass-enclosed courtyard where Belle was relaxing, stark naked, in her bath—the sarcophagus. She started out of it to receive him. Seeing him blush, she asked serenely, "Perhaps you would rather wait till the tide goes out?" Professor Norton fled.)

In 1892, Mrs. Jack tangled with the Empress Frederick of Germany over Susterman's *A Young Commander,* which she bought, thinking it a portrait of the Duke of Monmouth, from whom she claimed descent. Through Count Seckendorf in Berlin, the empress tried to get Belle to step aside and let her have the picture. Characteristically, Belle replied that her Stuart ancestry gave her as much right to it as the empress! Small wonder that when she sent a wreath to Liszt's funeral marked *Homage de l'Amerique,* it was placed alongside one from Queen Victoria.

The most notable sculpture at Fenway Court is Benvenuto Cellini's bronze bust of the art patron Bindo Altoviti. Michelangelo was not noted for his magnanimity toward other artists, but the museum quotes his letter praising this work, one of the two or three authentic Cellinis in America. The mosaic pavement in the center of the court at Fenway, said to be from the Villa Livia near Rome, is acknowledged as the finest example in the United States.

Perhaps the most astonishing single aspect of Fenway Court today is the disparity between its present value and what it cost Mrs. Gardner. Morris Carter, her biographer and the first curator of her collection, says, "What she paid was a minor consideration; she bought what she wanted and forgot what it cost." Despite this, she got an eye-popping series of bargains. Fenway Court and its collection cost her about $3,000,000, most of which she inherited from her father. Today it would probably not suffice to duplicate the building, and at present prices there are several of her top treasures that would bring more than that at auction. Carter says, "She professed not to value most expert opinion—she certainly had no use for pedantry; but she was in her own way a student, very well-read and very well-informed."

And she had superb advice, not only from the young Berenson but from Sargent (at whose suggestion she bought Tintoretto's *Lady in Black* from Prince Chigi's collection in Rome) and Whistler, as well as choice gifts from friends like Charles Eliot Norton and Thomas Whittemore. Belle once grandly explained that she could no longer afford second-rate pictures because she needed all her money for the first-rate. If she was apparently unaware of such distinguished contemporaries as Winslow Homer and Thomas Eakins, it is to her credit (or perhaps to Sargent's) that she ignored such fashionable painters as Bouguereau and the Barbizon school (who have become fasionable again, proably because of the dwindling supply of available works of better painters). Judged by comparison with the purchases of other pioneer American collectors of roughly the same vintage—W. W. Corcoran of the Corcoran Art Gallery in Washington and Henry Walters of the Walters Art Gallery in Baltimore—Mrs. Gardner's treasures stand up remarkably well. The late Francis Henry Taylor, director of New York's Metropolitan Museum, estimated that Walters and his son Henry spent $40,000,000 on their gallery, yet a long list of paintings they bought as works of Moro, Rembrandt, Goya, Hogarth, Gainsborough, and Constable have all had to be downgraded to "school of" pictures.

Belle seems to have known exactly what she wanted. For example, Sir Joseph Duveen, who later extracted astronomical prices from Frick, Mellon, and Kress for old masters, sold her only one picture—a portrait of a *Woman in Green and Crimson.* She bought it as an Antonio Pollaiuolo in 1907 through Berenson, but it later turned out to be the work of that artist's less well-known brother Piero. Berenson at that time was not yet a dean of art authorities, but a perceptive young man in his 30s, and he made an occasional mistake. The Velazquez *Pope Innocent X* that he and Mrs. Gardner agreed was "a whacker" is now "attributed to." In 1899, she bought at Berenson's suggestion what was thought to be the only existing portrait of Michelangelo, by Sebastiano del Piombo. When it was cleaned a few years later, it was found to be a self-portrait by Baccio Bandinelli, a rival sculptor.

Another disputed picture is *Young Lady of Fashion,* a girl with a pony-tail hairdo, now attributed to Paolo Uccello, but which Berenson insisted was the work of Domenico Veneziano. But the overwhelming majority of original attributions is still generally accepted.

A bowl of fresh violets (Belle's favorite flower), in accordance with her custom, is kept beside her favorite painting—a somewhat effeminate *Christ Carrying the Cross* that she bought as a Giorgione despite Berenson's advice: "Unquestionably genuine . . . a sublime illustration rather than a great work of art . . . not the kind of thing I think of for you." The picture still bears Giorgione's name, an attribution with which expert Lionello Venturi agreed, although Philip Hendy gives it to Palma Vecchio. However, an art gallery is not a barrel of apples, and a few disputed pictures do not spoil the many certified by Berenson that are precisely what they are represented to be.

"Love of art, not knowledge about art," says Morris Carter, "was her aim." All of Fenway Court is, as she intended, a mirror of her tastes and interests, and he adds, "Every detail speaks of the fun Mrs. Gardner had in doing it." This in itself was a fresh approach to custodianship of great art in America in the early years of this century. Belle personally supervised every detail of the construction from the day the ground was broken, when she found her first four-leaf clover. It is still preserved at Fenway in a crystal locket together with a relic of Saint Clare.

During the construction, she engaged a Boston building inspector in pitched battle with the haughty announcement that "It will be built as I wish." It was, too. Chauffeur-driven from Beacon Street daily, she brought her own lunch, contributed to the workmen's fund for beverages, and worked as hard as anybody on the job. Her favorite foreman was an Italian trumpet player named Bolgi. With him, she devised a system of alarms by which he sounded one toot on the trumpet for masons, two for steam fitters, three for plumbers, four for carpenters, and so on. She almost literally supervised the laying of every brick.

This Young Lady of Fashion *is now attributed to Paolo Uccello, but Berenson, who bought it for Mrs. Gardner, insisted it was by Veneziano.*

To get a desired wall color, she herself climbed the ladder, and dipping a sponge first in a pail of white paint and then of red, splashed it on. She once telephoned her architect's office that she had fired a plumber, adding that if another was not on the spot within the hour she'd get a new architect.

Before the opening night, she even pretested the acoustics of her Music Room before a foolproof audience—children from the Perkins Institution for the Blind. They came on a rainy afternoon, stacked their rubbers neatly where they could be found at the concert's end. An unthinking butler or footman scooped them all up from the hall and stacked them in a closet. The resulting confusion was something Belle remembered with horror for years afterward. As an old lady, when visitors came to see her collection, she sometimes asked them anxiously, "Have you got your rubbers?"

Crivelli's Saint George and the Dragon *was described as "drawn as if by lightning" by Bernard Berenson, who bought it for Mrs. Gardner.*

By this time, Mrs. Jack had become a living legend in Boston. The days when she, then Isabella Stewart, had been sent to Paris to finishing school seemed as remote in time as a Zurbaran. At the Paris school she met Back Bay's Julia Gardner; their fathers—two lonesome businessmen who were happy to be able to speak American to each other—also became friends. (Their mothers did not, but Mrs. Gardner, Senior, was a Peabody from Salem where it was "Peabody or Nobody.") Belle came to visit Julia in Boston, and her brother Jack fell madly in love with the guest—an infatuation from which he never recovered. Neither did the rest of the sedate Gardner clan. When Julia came to New York to return the visit, Mr. Stewart took the girls to a minstrel show, sending word backstage that he hoped there would be no coarse jokes that evening because Miss Gardner of Boston was in the house.

Belle was certainly no prude; she liked to tell risque jokes in mixed company. She disliked most women, anyway—a feeling many of them returned with interest—making only a few distinguished exceptions for opera stars Emma Eames and Nellie Melba and authors Edith Wharton and Julia Ward Howe. Belle preferred men and never made any secret of it. She had long since decided that "Money is the sixth sense which allows us to enjoy the other five," and there is little question that her money enhanced her charms for artists like Paderewski (who played for her privately—with a few friends hidden behind the arras), tenor Jean de Reszke (who always stayed for lunch if she promised him apple pie), and pianist-composer Ferruccio Busoni, to name only three. At a German spa, she acquired a photograph of Johann Strauss and Brahms, autographed by Strauss with a few bars from *The Blue Danube*. But of all men on earth, proper Bostonians were least likely to be impressed by her money or interested in it. For the most part, they had plenty of their own, but the roster of those she collected is astonishing—James Russell Lowell, Oliver Wendell Holmes, Henry L. Higginson (the father of the Boston Symphony, who wrote her concerning the acoustics of the new Symphony Hall), editor

Thomas Bailey Aldrich, and even starchy General Francis Walker (first president of the Massachusetts Institute of Technology, who playfully threatened to postpone a lecture series before the Lowell Institute to follow her to Washington for a cup of tea when she attended Cleveland's inauguration).

Social Boston's watchword was unostentatious good taste, but Belle loved display for its own sake. As a young matron she kept two footmen, when a single coachman was good enough for anybody else. A little later she maintained two adjacent houses on Beacon Street, which she connected with unexpected doorways. Her gowns came from Worth of London; asked if she burned them at the end of every season, Belle replied, "Don't spoil a good story by telling the truth." Even her carriages, which were usually driven faster than anybody else's, came from Binder of Paris. She was driving in one of them once when she was halted by a crowd of striking streetcar employees. An Irish voice, roaring out of the crowd, reassured her: "Don't be afraid, Mrs. Jack, I'll see you get through." It was John L. Sullivan. The crowd always seemed to sense that she was on their side. She was—although she claimed descent from the royal Stuarts of Scotland, and commemorated the execution of Charles I with a Mass in her private chapel. No true Boston blueblood would have relished so much a letter addressed only

> *Mrs. Gardner, Esq.*
> *well known lady in high life*
> *Boston, Mass.*

which reached its destination when a postal clerk scrawled across the envelope, "Try Mrs. Jack." This item is preserved at Fenway Court, along with correspondence from George Santayana, Richard Mansfield, Owen Wister, Richard Harding Davis, and William Dean Howells, along with photographs and autographs of such artists as Fritz Kreisler and Pavlova.

And Belle was God's gift to newspapermen in search of copy. "No woman in Boston," wrote one, "has been so much discussed, both privately and publicly. Mrs. Gardner really does more for the entertainment of Boston society than anyone else, for she not only entertains her friends, but her vagaries entertain the world at large." Belle knew as she read this that by tradition a Boston lady gets her name in print three times—at her birth, her wedding, and her funeral. To most of the Gardners except her husband, Belle was a hussy. The dislike was mutual. Asked for a donation to Boston's Charitable Eye and Ear Infirmary, she snapped that she didn't know there was a charitable eye or ear in Boston.

Her European travels began on doctor's orders soon after the Civil War (which she later said she was too young to remember), not long after her only son, Jackie, died in infancy. She was, or said she was, so ill she had to be carried aboard ship on a stretcher. Given to seasickness, she subsisted on champagne and biscuits, but on arrival found she was well enough to trek across Russia to Moscow and St. Petersburg. Under Sargent's tutelage, Spain had a special fascination for her, but she loved to travel everywhere. A series of lectures on Oriental art in her own Beacon Street home inspired her to make a world tour with her husband. Although two carriages full of flowers followed them to the station when they left, it seems unlikely that any of them came from the ladies of Boston; Belle probably sent most of them herself from her own greenhouses. She toured Angkor Vat, which had been discovered only a few years previously. At another Cambodian ruin, Belle, whose favorite dish was cold corned beef and who adored beer, had champagne for breakfast, and noted in her diary that she "ate my first peacock."

Some of Belle's antics did her little credit. It is hard to explain why she thought it necessary to feel the flexed biceps of Sandow the Great, or her playfulness with lions at the Boylston Street Zoo. She once took two cubs driving in her carriage; one returned wearing a big bow of ribbon as a mark of her favor. On another occasion she narrowly escaped being clawed by the mother of three cubs. On still another, she took a ferocious-looking but perfectly harmless old lion for a stroll on a leash, to the consternation of other zoo visitors.

Given to the theatrical gesture, Belle once stepped up to soprano Nellie Melba after a concert at Fenway Court and removed a huge yellow diamond from her hand. "This was coveted by the King of Cambodia," she declaimed, "but I have saved it for the Queen of Song!" This was pure corn and as carefully calculated in advance as the orchids on the palm trees at Fenway Court, but it made wonderful newspaper copy.

Then there was her famous penance. Attended by her liveried footman and coachman, she drove up before the fashionable Church of the Advent just as Sunday morning services were about to begin. The footman filled a pail with hot water at a nearby mansion. Belle, traditionally decked out in sackcloth and ashes, swabbed down the steps on her hands and knees with laundry soap and water. This accomplished, she handed bucket and brush back to the footman, stepped back into her barouche, and clattered regally away.

The last of the great entertainments at Fenway Court took place in 1908, but the epilogue to the story of "America's most fascinating widow" was long and perhaps a little sad. Like many rich people, she became exceedingly stingy about small things in her last years. One lamb chop per person was the rule at luncheon. When Morris Carter says wryly that the statues of Saint George and Saint Florian which flanked the entrance were her guardians against fire and theft that saved her the expense of insurance, he is putting the facts about her $3,000,000 investment in a polite light. The servants complained that they didn't get enough to eat; Belle's friends actually feared that she herself was undernourished.

In *Rumor and Reflection,* Bernard Berenson recalled his patron: "When her husband died, and the bills of the baker and butcher and electrician were brought to her, she got into a panic from which she never quite recovered. She who in Europe had traveled like royalty . . . now went second class, and, frequenting the same hotels as before, would take the cheapest rooms and order the least expensive dishes." Rudolph Elie, Boston columnist and music critic, tells of a student who was asked to dinner, called for in a chauffeur-driven car, and taken to Childs.

Jack Gardner once said that Belle never really grew up, but she had plenty of time for reflection now—remembering an afternoon with Monet at Giverny; the day in Paris when Massenet played his new opera for her; a lecture at Fenway by Lady Gregory on the Abbey Theatre; one of Isadora Duncan's rare Boston appearances; Busoni playing at a birthday party for Anders Zorn; Edward MacDowell in Beacon Street . . . the list was endless. In 1919, Mrs. Gardner suffered a stroke. Thereafter she was carried about her palace in a gondola chair from Venice, her "home from home" which she would never see again.

If Belle Gardner devoted her life to pleasure, in accordance with her motto, it was surely no accident that she left her palace "for education and enjoyment of the public." And, in that order, that is precisely what Fenway Court has offered more than 60,000 visitors a year for more than half a century (in recent years, it has been approximately 165,000). Mrs. Jack was a kind of John the Baptist for a great many modern museum techniques—the incorporation of authentic architectural details in the building, dramatic lighting of important pictures, paintings shown in rooms appropriate to the period in which they were created. She did not foresee the great traffic between museums in the borrowing and lending of paintings for special exhibitions—the principal means by which they call attention to themselves and build attendance. Nothing may be borrowed from the Gardner, nor does it ever ask for the loan of anything. Only a regular concert series gets its name briefly into the news. But with or without publicity, it is well worth seeing, both as a mirror and memorial to a fascinating woman and one of America's truly great collections of art.

Nelson Lansdale, a free-lance writer, was formerly art and music editor of Newsweek.

Volume 11

ENCYCLOPEDIC SECTION

The two-page reference guide below lists the entries by categories. The entries in this section supplement the subject matter covered in the text of this volume. A **cross-reference** (*see*) means that a separate entry appears elsewhere in this section. However, certain important persons and events mentioned here have individual entries in the Encyclopedic Section of another volume. Consult the Index in Volume 18.

AMERICAN POLITICAL LEADERS

George Hearst
George Hoar
Robert G. Ingersoll

Thomas B. Reed
Philetus Sawyer
William Marcy Tweed
Lew Wallace

ARTISTS AND ARCHITECTS

Nathaniel Currier
Daniel Chester French
Winslow Homer
Richard Morris Hunt
James Merritt Ives
William Jenney

Frederick Law Olmsted
Albert Pinkham Ryder
Augustus Saint-Gaudens
John Singer Sargent
Louis Sullivan
James McNeill Whistler

BUSINESS AND INVENTION

Atlantic cable
James Gordon Bennett, Jr.
Diamond Jim Brady
Currier and Ives
Charles A. Dana

Abner Doubleday
Cyrus Field
George Hearst
Adolph S. Ochs
Joseph Pulitzer
Henry Walters

JOURNALISM

James Gordon Bennett, Jr.
Nellie Bly
Elizabeth Cochrane
Stephen Crane
Charles A. Dana
George Hearst

Adolph S. Ochs
Joseph Pulitzer
Jacob Riis
Henry M. Stanley
Bayard Taylor
Theodore Tilton
Charles Dudley Warner

LITERATURE

Henry Adams
William Taylor Adams
Horatio Alger, Jr.
Edward Bellamy
George Washington Cable
Samuel Clemens
Stephen Crane
Emily Dickinson
May Wilkins Freeman
Hamlin Garland
Joel Chandler Harris
Bret Harte
William Dean Howells
Henry James

Sarah Orne Jewett
Henry Wadsworth Longfellow
James Russell Lowell
Frank Norris
Oliver Optic
Thomas Nelson Page
Vernon L. Parrington
Bayard Taylor
Mark Twain
Lew Wallace
Charles Dudley Warner
Edith Wharton
Walt Whitman
Owen Wister

REFORM LEADERS AND MOVEMENTS

Jane Addams
Edward Bellamy
George Washington Cable
Elizabeth Cochrane
Theodore Cuyler
John Dewey
Richard T. Ely
George Hoar
Hull House
Dwight Lyman Moody

Carrie Nation
National Woman Suffrage Association
Nineteenth Amendment
Jacob Riis
Josiah Strong
T. De Witt Talmage
Theodore Tilton
Booker T. Washington
Frances E. Willard
Woman's Christian Temperance Union

THOUGHT AND CULTURE

Albert
baseball
Edwin Booth
Phillips Brooks
Buffalo Bill
William F. Cody
Russell H. Conwell
Theodore Cuyler
John Dewey
Abner Doubleday
Richard T. Ely

John Fiske
Isabella Stewart Gardner
Oliver Wendell Holmes
Robert G. Ingersoll
William James
James Russell Lowell
Annie Oakley
Vernon L. Parrington
Josiah Strong
John L. Sullivan
Victoria
Henry Walters

A

ADAMS, Henry Brooks (1838–1918). This noted Boston-born historian and writer was the descendant of one of the most famous families in American history. His great-grandfather was John Adams (1735–1826), the second President of the United States. His grandfather was John Quincy Adams (1767–1848), the nation's sixth President, and his father was Charles Francis Adams (1807–1886), a distinguished statesman who was ambassador to Great Britain from 1861 to 1868. After graduating from Harvard College in 1858, Henry Adams toured Europe and then lived in England, where he served as his father's secretary and also found time to contribute articles to various American periodicals. He settled in Washington, D. C., in 1868, where he continued his journalistic activities. However, Adams was dissatisfied with life in the nation's capital during the corrupt administration of President Ulysses S. Grant (1822–1885). He left the capital, and from 1870 to 1877 he taught medieval, American, and European history at Harvard and also edited (1869–1876) the scholarly *North American Review*. Missing his role as "stable-companion to statesmen," Adams returned to Washington in 1877. There, he published biographies of financier Albert Gallatin (1761–1849) in 1879 and statesman John Randolph (1773–1833) three years later. Adams also wrote two novels that were published anonymously—*Democracy* (1880), a description of post-Civil War Washington politics, and *Esther* (1884), which was about New York society. He then completed his nine-volume *History of the United States During the Administrations of Thomas Jefferson and James Madison* (1889–1891), the first six chapters of which are still considered to be an unsurpassed analysis of the intellectual, economic, and social climate in America at the beginning of the 19th century. A turning point in Adams' career occurred during one of his trips abroad in 1895. During a stay in France that summer, he went to see two masterpieces of medieval architecture, the abbey of Mont-Saint-Michel and Chartres Cathedral. To Adams, the buildings represented the sense of unity characteristic of the 13th century, when man was the center of the universe, unified by religion. Later, an electrical dynamo he saw at the Paris Exposition in 1900 impressed him as a mechanistic symbol of what he believed was a fragmented and aimless contemporary society. He made these experiences the basis of a new historical theory, in which he measured the life and thought of various eras in terms of the dominant forces of those periods. He expressed this theory in two brilliant books, *Mont-Saint-Michel and Chartres: A Study in Thirteenth-Century Unity* (1904), and *The Education of Henry Adams: A Study in Twentieth-Century Multiplicity* (1907). Together, these volumes explain Adams' contention that modern man, no longer at the center of his universe, has a special need to create unity out of complexity. Adams' other works include the essay "A Letter to American Teachers of History" (1910), in which he predicted that in the future the interpretation of history would be based on laws of physics.

ADAMS, William Taylor. *See* **Optic, Oliver.**

ADDAMS, Jane (1860–1935). This humanitarian reformer founded Chicago's famed Hull

Jane Addams founded the first settlement house, Hull House, in 1889.

House, one of the first social settlements in the nation dedicated to improving the lives of slum dwellers. Born in Illinois, Miss Addams graduated from Rockford College in 1881 and attended the Women's Medical College in Philadelphia until her health failed in 1882. During her convalescence, she traveled in England, where she became acquainted with the social-welfare programs sponsored by Toynbee Hall, a London settlement, and subsequently decided to devote her life to bettering the conditions of poor people. In 1889, Miss Addams and a friend, Ellen Gates Starr (1860–1940), rented the old Hull mansion in a slum district of Chicago and opened it as Hull House. As its director, Miss Addams soon won the trust of the people in the neighborhood, giving them a sense of civic pride by providing playgrounds, day nurseries, clinics, and adult-education courses for immigrants. By 1905, she had financed and built the finest educational and recreational facilities for the working classes in the nation. The outstanding artists and educators attracted to Hull House conducted a cultural program that included a labor museum, a music school, and a theatrical group. In 1915, Miss Addams became involved in the movement for international peace, which she believed was not merely the absence of war, but "the nurture of human life." For her efforts to outlaw war, she was one of the recipients of the Nobel Peace Prize in 1931. Among the many books she wrote in her lifetime, the most famous was *Twenty Years at Hull House* (1910), which remains a classic on social rehabilitation and reform.

ALBERT. *See* **Victoria.**

ALGER, Horatio, Jr. (1834–1899). America's most popular author of juvenile fiction, Horatio Alger wrote stories of success that made his name synonymous with finding fame and fortune through hard work, clean living, and dogged determination. About 20,000,000 copies of his more than 100 boys' books have been sold. Alger was born in Revere, Massachusetts. His father, a minister, was smug, pompous, and rigidly puritanical. As a boy, Alger was nicknamed Holy Horatio. After graduating from Harvard College in 1852 and the Harvard Divinity School in 1860, Alger rebelliously fled to Paris, where he spent a year living like a bohemian. Repenting, Alger returned home and entered the ministry in 1864. Two years later, he went to New York, where he served as chaplain of the Newsboys' Lodging House and began his writing career. The *Ragged Dick* series, his most popular, began appearing in 1867, the *Luck and Pluck* series in 1869, and the *Tattered Tom* series in 1871. Alger also wrote biographies of poor boys who had achieved financial and social respectability, including *Abraham Lincoln, the Backwoods Boy* (1883). Alger seldom used a simple word if he could think of a flowery one. His barbers were "knights of the scissors" and his liquor "a poisonous decoction." Alger longed to write serious adult fiction but never succeeded. He died in poverty, having squandered all his money.

ATLANTIC CABLE. *See* **Field, Cyrus.**

B

BASEBALL. *See* **Doubleday, Abner.**

BELLAMY, Edward (1850–1898). A famous Massachusetts-born novelist and social reformer, Bellamy first gained international acclaim in 1888, when he published *Looking Backward; 2000–1887,* a utopian romance. In it, he described an ideal world in A.D. 2000, in which poverty, crime, advertising, and many diseases have been eradicated through the replacement of private enterprise by a democratic form of capitalism in which all citizens share the wealth and industry of the nation. After touring Europe in 1868, Bellamy returned to America, where he became a lawyer, but he never practiced law. He worked instead as a journalist, and in 1880 he helped found the Springfield (Massachusetts) *Daily News.* However, his main interest was creative writing, and in 1879 he began the serial publication of *The Duke of Stockbridge,* a historical romance dealing with Shays' Rebellion of 1786–1787. He never finished this novel, which was completed and published by a cousin in 1900. Bellamy also wrote short stories for magazines that were later collected under the title *The Blind Man's World and Other Stories* (1898). Three works—*Six to One: A Nantucket Idyl* (1878), in which Bellamy reflected about a voyage he took to Hawaii in 1877, and two psychological novels, *Dr. Heidenhoff's Process* (1880) and *Miss Ludington's Sister* (1884)—were written before the publication of *Looking Backward* in 1888. This work, which is still widely read today, inspired the formation of Bellamy Clubs, the Nationalist Party, and the monthly magazine *Nationalist* (1888–1891), all of which popularized and advocated Bellamy's social theories. Bellamy also founded and edited the *New Nation* (1891-1894), a weekly that advanced his ideas. In 1897, he published *Equality,* a sequel to *Looking Backward* that provided a more theoretical treatment of his social concepts.

BENNETT, James Gordon, Jr. (1841-1918). Succeeding his father, James Gordon Bennett (1795-1872), as publisher of the New York *Herald*, Bennett continued that great paper's tradition of aggressive journalism, while establishing a personal reputation as a playboy. Bennett was educated by private tutors and at the Ecole Polytechnique in Paris. He returned to America in 1861 and served in the navy during the Civil War. In 1866, Bennett became managing editor of the *Herald*. Anticipating the trend toward afternoon newspapers, Bennett founded the *Evening Telegram* in 1869. That same year, he sent **Henry Stanley** (*see*), one of his reporters, to find Dr. David Livingstone (1813-1873), who had been lost in Africa. Stanley's two-year adventure, reported exclusively in the *Herald,* was the sensation of the day. Bennett later financed unsuccessful expeditions to find a northwest passage (1875) and to the Arctic (1879-1881). Together with financier John W. Mackay (1831-1902), he founded the Commercial Cable Company. It laid two transatlantic cables to Europe, a feat that enabled the *Herald* to achieve preeminence in foreign-news reporting. Bennett established a Paris edition of the daily *Herald* in 1887. By the turn of the century, however, the *Herald* faced stiff competition from the *World* owned by **Joseph Pulitzer,** the *Times* under **Adolph Ochs** (*see both*), and the *Journal* under William Randolph Hearst (1863-1951). The *Herald*'s circulation and advertising

began to decline. Meanwhile, Bennett had been living in Paris and directing his staff by cable since 1877. That year, his engagement to the daughter of a prominent Washington family had been broken abruptly for reasons never disclosed. When the girl's brother struck Bennett with a horsewhip, Bennett challenged him to a duel. Shots were harmlessly exchanged, but the ensuing scandal caused Bennett to leave the country and take up residence in Paris. There, he became a prominent figure in society. He entered yacht races and donated cups for balloon, yacht, automobile, and airplane racing. He was responsible for introducing polo in the United States. It has been estimated that Bennett spent more than $30,000,000 on his personal pleasures while owner of the *Herald*. In 1924, six years after he died, the paper merged with the New York *Tribune*.

BLY, Nellie. *See* **Cochrane, Elizabeth.**

BOOTH, Edwin (1833-1893). Hailed by most critics as the greatest American actor of the 19th century, Booth specialized in Shakespearean roles. He was a member of a well-known acting family, which included his brother John Wilkes Booth (1838-1865), the assassin of President Abraham Lincoln (1809-1865). His father, Junius Brutus Booth (1796-1852), was a noted actor whose performances were somewhat erratic because of his heavy drinking. As a child, Booth accompanied his father on performing tours to take care of him. In 1849, he made his first stage appearance in a minor role in *Richard III.* Two years later, Booth took the lead role in the same play when his

The Booth brothers—John Wilkes, Edwin, and Junius Brutus—appeared together for the first time in 1864.

father was unable to go on. Booth then toured California, the Sandwich Islands (Hawaii), and Australia. He returned east in 1857 and was an immediate success on the stage. In the 1864-1865 season, Booth played a record 100 consecutive performances of *Hamlet* at the Winter Garden Theatre in New York. He had a restrained, natural style, which was in contrast with the shouting and bombast of his father's day. In addition, Booth abandoned the abridged and rewritten versions of Shakespeare's plays that were generally performed in those days, presenting instead the authentic texts. Deeply distressed over his brother's assassination of the President in April, 1865, Booth retired from the stage. He returned in 1866, and after a fire destroyed the Winter Garden Theatre, built Booth's Theatre, which opened in 1869. For four seasons, the theater was known as the showplace of American drama, but the Panic of 1873 sent

Booth into bankruptcy. He became a traveling actor once again and, despite ill health, remained one of the greatest performers of his day. In 1879, a lunatic fired at Booth twice during a performance of *Richard II* in Chicago, but he remained on the stage. In 1888, Booth founded The Players, a private New York men's club that sought to raise the prestige of the theater to the same level as that of literature, music, and the other fine arts. Booth lived at the club from his retirement in 1891 until his death. Today, the club, whose membership includes actors, writers, critics, directors, and theater historians, houses one of the finest collections of dramatic literature and art in the nation.

BRADY, James Buchanan ("Diamond Jim") (1856–1917). Brady made a fortune selling railroad equipment and dealing in rail stocks, and in the early 1890s he said, "Hell, I'm rich. It's time I had some fun." He did. The value of Brady's diamond and jewel collection was estimated at $2,000,000, and he was one of the best-known men in New York night-life circles. Brady had started as a bellboy in a hotel. He worked at several jobs for the New York Central Railroad, and in 1879 he took a job as a salesman for a manufacturer of railroad equipment. Brady was a huge success and became an officer of several corporations connected with railroading. He was seen often at elaborate New York dinner parties, wearing diamonds from his collection, or cycling in Central Park on one of his jewel-studded bicycles. Brady once presented the famous actress Lillian Russell (1861–1922) with a $1,900 bicycle so that she might accompany him. In 1912, he contributed funds to establish the James Buchanan Brady Urological Institute at Johns Hopkins Hospital in Baltimore.

BROOKS, Phillips (1835–1893). Brooks, who was consecrated Episcopal bishop of Massachusetts in 1891, was a well-known preacher and the author of the popular Christmas hymn *O Little Town of Bethlehem* (1868). Born in Boston, Brooks graduated from Harvard College in 1855. He then studied at the Episcopal Seminary in Alexandria, Virginia, and was ordained a deacon in 1859. During the next 10 years, he was a rector in Philadelphia, first of the Church of the Advent and then of Holy Trinity Church. From 1869 until 1891, Brooks was rector of the fashionable Trinity Church in Boston. In 1877, he delivered a series of lectures at Yale Divinity School. Published as *Lectures on Preaching* that same year, they contained his famous statement that preaching was "the bringing of truth through personality." Two years later in Philadelphia, Brooks delivered a series of lectures that were published as *The Influence of Jesus* (1879). On July 4, 1880, he gave the sermon at London's Westminster Abbey, and the following Sunday he had the honor to be the first American invited by Queen Victoria (*see*) to preach before her at the Royal Chapel of Windsor Castle.

BUFFALO BILL. *See* **Cody, William F.**

C

CABLE, George Washington (1844–1925). A native of New Orleans, Cable is best known for his colorful short stories and novels dealing with the Creoles of Louisiana (*see pp. 968–969*). Together with **Bret Harte** (*see*), he popularized the movement in American fiction to depict the life and customs of a region. Cable served two years in a Confederate cavalry regiment and during his free time taught himself mathematics and Latin. He contracted malaria just after the war's end. During his two-year recuperation, Cable began a weekly column for the New Orleans *Picayune*. Its success won him a post as a staff reporter, but being a devout Calvinist, he refused to enter theaters to review plays and was dismissed. He then got a job as a clerk and taught himself French, studied the New Orleans archives, and continued his writing. A literary scout for *Scribner's Monthly* discovered him, and after a number of Cable's short stories had appeared in the journal, they were published in 1879 as a collection entitled *Old Creole Days*. The *Grandissimes*, his first novel, appeared the following year. Cable became increasingly interested in reform, and he advocated improved prison conditions and better treatment of blacks in *The Silent South* (1885). The book, which was a compilation of a series of articles on reform, aroused resentment in the South. Shortly afterward, Cable moved to Northampton, Massachusetts, where he founded the Home-Culture Clubs, which later became the Northampton People's Institute. For a time, he toured the nation with **Mark Twain** (*see*), reading his own works before large audiences. Cable's continuing interest in reform led to the publication of *The Negro Question* (1888) and *The Southern Struggle for Pure Government* (1890). From 1901 to 1918, he returned to writing fiction and published six more novels dealing with the Creoles. Although popular with the public, these books did not win the critical acclaim of his earlier works.

CENTRAL PARK. *See* **Olmsted, Frederick Law.**

CLEMENS, Samuel. *See* **Twain, Mark.**

COCHRANE, Elizabeth (1867–1922). This journalist, who wrote under the by-line of Nellie (or Nelly) Bly—a name taken from a popular song by Stephen Foster (1826–1864)—achieved international renown for her sensational reporting on social abuses of the day and for her voyage around the world in record time. Born in Cochran Mills, Pennsylvania, she moved to Pittsburgh about 1881 and began her newspaper career on the staff of the *Dispatch*. She was dubbed with the pseudonym Nellie Bly and advanced from writing about the plight of Pittsburgh working girls to being society editor in charge of art and drama. In 1888, Nellie was employed by the New York *World,* owned by **Joseph Pulitzer** (*see*), and then assigned to investigate the treatment of the insane on Blackwell's Island (now Welfare Island) in New York. By feigning insanity for half a dozen doctors, Nellie was admitted to the asylum, where she spent 10 days observing the squalid conditions there. Upon her release, she published an account that led to a grand-jury investigation. The following year, the *World* dispatched Nellie around the world to see if she could travel faster than the hero of *Around the World in 80 Days,* a science-fiction novel by Jules Verne (1828–1905). She made the trip in what was then a phenomenal 72 days,

Elizabeth Cochrane

6 hours, and 11 minutes. Nellie married an elderly barrel manufacturer, Robert Seaman, in 1895, and after his death in 1904 supervised his company's finances. However, tricked by employees and pressured by creditors, she lost the company. At the time of her death, she was on the staff of the New York *Evening Journal.*

CODY, William F. ("Buffalo Bill") (1846–1917). Buffalo Bill Cody was a renowned frontier scout, buffalo hunter, and showman. When only 11 years old, the Iowa-born youngster took a job as a "cavvy boy" in charge of saddle horses in an army supply train. He was later employed as a rider by a freighting firm to carry packages through Indian country. In 1859, Cody joined other prospectors in the Denver gold strike. He worked briefly the following year as a rider for the Pony Express. During the Civil War, Cody became a scout for the Ninth Kansas Cavalry in that unit's campaign against the Comanches and Kiowas. He enlisted as a scout in the regular army in 1864. He was hired three years later by a firm of food contractors to supply buffalo meat to

railroad-construction camps. In one day, Cody killed 69 buffalo; in one season, 4,862. His skill as a hunter earned him the nickname Buffalo Bill. After 1868, Cody again served as an army scout. In 1872, he made an appearance on the stage in a play written by his friend, Edward Z. C. Judson (1823–1886), who wrote under the name of Ned Buntline. Cody became chief scout for the Fifth Cavalry during the Sioux War of 1876. He killed Yellow Hand, son of a Cheyenne chief, in a famous face-to-face encounter at War Bonnet Creek. In 1883, Cody organized his celebrated Wild West show, an exhibition of cowboys, Indians, and sharpshooting frontiersmen (*see pp. 940–941*). He hired **Annie Oakley** (*see*) as a star attraction two

William F. Cody

years later. The show toured America and Europe successfully until 1916. Cody invested his vast earnings in ranch properties near North Platte, Nebraska, and Cody, Wyoming. According to his wishes, he was buried on the top of Lookout Mountain, near Golden, Colorado.

CONWELL, Russell H. (1843–1925). A Baptist minister, Conwell became celebrated for his lecture "Acres of Diamonds," in which he preached that poverty was a sin when wealth was so easy to attain. The clergyman, a native of Massachusetts, studied law at Yale and later at the Albany Law School. In 1862, during the Civil War, he recruited a company of volunteers in Massachusetts. After the war, Conwell moved to Minneapolis. There, he established a law practice and founded a newspaper, the *Daily Chronicle*. Failing health prompted him to accept a position abroad, and he went to Germany in 1867 as immigration agent for the state of Minnesota. Having recovered his health, Conwell settled in Boston and resumed the practice of law in 1870. Although an atheist in college, Conwell had become religious during the war and afterward studied for the ministry while practicing law in Boston. In 1879, he was ordained a minister of the Baptist Church. Less than two years later, Conwell was asked to accept the parish of the debt-ridden Grace Baptist Church in Philadelphia. Under his direction, the church not only paid its debts but prospered as well. In 1891, the congregation moved to spacious new quarters in the Baptist Temple, with Conwell as pastor. There, he established a night school in the basement. Out of these evening classes grew Temple University,

a college for laboring people. Conwell also founded Samaritan Hospital in Philadelphia that same year. A popular orator as well as preacher, Conwell delivered his famous address, "Acres of Diamonds," more than 5,000 times. The lecture expressed the view that opportunity was available and had only to be seized. The speech reflected the materialistic ideals of his generation. Among the books Conwell wrote were *Lessons in Travel* (1870), *Present Successful Opportunities* (1878), and *Borrowed Ayes* (1923).

CRANE, Stephen (1871–1900). A novelist, short-story writer, and war correspondent, Crane

Stephen Crane

was the author of *The Red Badge of Courage,* which is considered one of the finest war novels ever written. This New Jersey-born writer briefly attended Lafayette College in Pennsylvania and Syracuse University in New York.

At college, he had drafted his first novel, *Maggie: A Girl of the Streets*. As with some of his later works, Crane used his imagination to create the conditions of life about which he had no or little experience. In 1891, he settled in New York City and worked as a free-lance reporter for the *Tribune* and the *Herald*. Crane's life for the next five years was a struggle against poverty. Often hungry and ill, the young writer spent much time in the slums of the city. He completed *Maggie* and published it at his own expense in 1893. Two years later, *The Red Badge of Courage* appeared. The book was a spectacular critical success and brought Crane immediate fame. A novel of the Civil War, *The Red Badge* accurately describes the psychology of the common soldier in battle. The vivid realism of the book set new standards in descriptive writing and was an influence on later novelists. In 1896, Crane joined an illegal expedition to encourage rebellion in Cuba. His ship was wrecked off the Florida coast, and the writer and several companions were cast adrift in a rowboat. The adventure supplied Crane with the material for one of his best short stories, "The Open Boat," published in a collection entitled *The Open Boat, and Other Tales of Adventure* (1898). In 1897, he went to Greece as a war correspondent. The following year, he covered the Spanish-American War in Cuba. Crane spent the last two years of his life in England, where he became friendly with **Henry James** (*see*) and Joseph Conrad (1857–1924). He died of tuberculosis while on a trip to the Black Forest in Germany. Crane's other works included *Active Service* (1899) and *Wounds in the Rain* (1900).

Among his volumes of verse are *The Black Riders and Other Lines* (1895) and *War is Kind* (1899).

CURRIER, Nathaniel. *See* **Currier and Ives.**

CURRIER AND IVES. In an age when photography was still in its infancy and newspapers carried few, if any, illustrations, the lithographic firm of Currier and Ives brought the happenings and scenes of contemporary 19th-century life into hundreds of thousands of American homes. The firm was founded in 1835 in New York City by Nathaniel Currier (1813–1881), a Massachusetts lithographer. About 15 years later, Currier hired a self-educated artist, James Merritt Ives (1824–1895), as a bookkeeper. The two men became partners in 1857, and thereafter all their lithographs carried the name of Currier and Ives. These were chiefly illustrations of national disasters such as wrecks and fires. The firm first established a nationwide reputation when it published a lithograph of the burning of the steamboat *Lexington* in 1840. The subjects depicted by Currier and Ives later included social, political, and sporting scenes (*see pp. 919–925*). In all, more than 7,000 lithographs were issued. They sold at prices ranging up to $3 each, depending on size. The lithographs were printed in black and white on hand-operated presses and then colored by a staff of a dozen women. Currier retired from the firm in 1880. Ives continued until his death in 1895. Their sons, Edward W. Currier and Chauncey Ives, carried on the business for some time, then sold their interest, and the firm closed in 1907. Its prints are now collectors' items.

CUYLER, Theodore (1822–1909). As the minister of the Lafayette Avenue Presbyterian Church in Brooklyn, Cuyler gained an international reputation as a Christian speaker and writer. During his lifetime, he published 22 books and more than 3,000 articles. Influenced by his deeply religious mother, Cuyler graduated from Princeton in 1841 and from Princeton Theological Seminary five years later. In 1860, after serving in several New Jersey churches, he became minister of the Lafayette Church, a position he held for 30 years. In his sermons, Cuyler claimed to have found that "the true things were not new, and most of the new things were not true." He was active in the temperance movement, was in great demand as a public speaker, and wrote continually for the religious press. Many of his articles were translated into foreign languages. Cuyler resigned from the Lafayette Church in 1890 to devote all his time to writing. His books included *Stirring the Eagle's Nest and other Practical Discourses* (1892), *Recollections of a Long Life* (1902), and *A Model Christian* (1903).

D

DANA, Charles Anderson (1819–1897). A famous newspaperman, Dana was editor of the New York *Sun* for nearly 30 years. He summed up its editorial policy in saying, "It will study condensation, clearness, point, and will endeavor to present its daily photograph of the whole world's doings in the most luminous and lively manner." Born in New Hampshire, Dana entered Harvard College in 1839 and two years later joined the Brook Farm experiment in communal living,

Charles A. Dana

staying until 1846. The following year, he joined the staff of the New York *Tribune* at $14 a week and for most of the following 15 years was its managing editor. He resigned in 1862 because the *Tribune*'s editor, Horace Greeley (1811–1872), considered his attitude toward the Civil War too militant. Dana subsequently worked for the War Department, where he was one of the first to recognize the military abilities of General Ulysses S. Grant (1822–1885). From 1864 to 1865, Dana served as Assistant Secretary of War. In 1868, he paid $175,000 to purchase part ownership of the *Sun*. The paper became enormously successful under his editorship (*see p. 939*), although Dana himself grew notorious for his support of some of the most corrupt politicians of Tammany Hall and for his opposition to any social reforms. Taking as his motto the phrase, "If you see it in the *Sun,* it's so," he enlivened its news pages with his concise, lively, and often cynical style. He made the *Sun* a witty and enjoyable paper that emphasized human interest features, amply covered crime stories, and was famous for its catchy headlines. The *Sun* became known as the newspaperman's newspaper because of its vivid writing and because it employed a staff of the best journalists of the day, including **Jacob Riis** (*see*). Dana described his war experiences in *Recollection of the Civil War* (1898). He was co-editor, with the social reformer and literary critic George Ripley (1802–1880), of the 16-volume *New American Cyclopaedia* (1858–1863). Dana also wrote *The Art of Newspaper Making* (1895) and *Eastern Journeys* (1898).

DEWEY, John (1859–1952). This famous Vermont-born philosopher and educator was a pioneer in the field of progressive education. Dewey was an exponent of pragmatism, a philosophy developed by **William James** (*see*). He also devised his own philosophical system, called Instrumentalism, which held that man and the things around him are in a constant state of change. Thus, he said, human thoughts, activities, and institutions must change constantly in order for men to understand and control the world. Similarly, truth is not a constant value, he maintained, but is based on human experience and may be explored and understood through investigation. This philosophy led Dewey to reject authoritarian teaching methods and to advocate progressive education—that is, learning by doing. Dewey opposed totalitarian forms of government and was a firm believer in democracy. He participated in movements to strengthen social welfare, to bring about political reform, and to protect academic freedom. Dewey was graduated from the University of Vermont in 1879 and five years later received his doctoral degree from Johns Hopkins University. He subsequently taught philosophy at the Universities of Michigan (1884–1888

and 1889–1894), Minnesota (1888–1889), and Chicago (1894–1904). At Chicago, he was director of the School of Education (1902–1904). Dewey also taught at Columbia University in New York City from 1904 to 1930. Absent-minded, Dewey was often a day late or a day early for his lectures. He liked to read detective novels. Although his philosophy was basically simple, his explanations were so obscure that they had to be clarified by many writers. Often called the dean of American philosophers, Dewey wrote on almost all fields of philosophy except metaphysics. Among the most famous of his numerous writings are *Psychology* (1887), *The Child and the Curriculum* (1902), *Democracy and Education* (1916), *Reconstruction in Philosophy* (1920), *Liberalism and Social Action* (1935), and *Problems of Men* (1946).

DICKINSON, Emily (1830–1886). A recluse who spent most of her life in her native Amherst,

CULVER PICTURES

Emily Dickinson

Massachusetts, Miss Dickinson is considered one of the greatest woman poets in history. She wrote poems that were brief but pointed, usually mixing abstract concepts, such as nature, love, death, and immortality, with concrete images from the everyday world, as in her famous verse "The Chariot": "*Because I could not stop for Death,/He kindly stopped for me;/The carriage held but just ourselves/ And Immortality.*" The daughter of a prominent lawyer, Miss Dickinson completed her education by studying (1847–1848) at Mount Holyoke Female Seminary (now Mount Holyoke College) in South Hadley, Massachusetts. Her subsequent life was outwardly uneventful. In 1854, she visited Washington, D. C., and Philadelphia with her family. Shortly after her return home, she withdrew to the seclusion of her family's mansion for the rest of her life. Because she always dressed in white, Miss Dickinson soon became known as The Nun of Amherst. Some historians believe that this self-imposed withdrawal was caused by her love for a married clergyman whom she had met on her trip to Philadelphia. Although she wrote more than 1,700 poems, only a few were published while she was alive, and her poetic genius went unrecognized until the publication after her death of *Poems* (1890) and *Poems: Second Series* (1891). Both collections were compiled and to some extent rewritten by Thomas Wentworth Higginson (1823–1911), a clergyman and writer, and Mabel Loomis Todd (1856–1932), an author and friend of Miss Dickinson. Several badly edited volumes of her works by other writers were published before the 1950s, when Thomas H. Johnson edited the definitive three-volume *Poems of Emily Dickinson* (1955) and the three-volume collection of her *Letters* (1958).

DOUBLEDAY, Abner (1819–1893). As a schoolboy in Cooperstown, New York, Doubleday invented the modern game of baseball. The rudiments of the sport already existed—many kinds of bat-and-ball games were played—but in 1835 Doubleday devised the diamond-shaped playing field, assigned players to specific positions (his teams had 11 men rather than today's nine), and named the sport baseball. Doubleday's career, however, was not in athletics but in the military service. A native of Ballston Spa, New York, he graduated from West Point in 1842. He served throughout the Mexican War and then fought against the Seminole Indians in Florida. As a captain stationed at Fort Sumter, South Carolina, in April, 1861, Doubleday aimed the first Union shot in response to the Confederate attack that started the Civil War. By early 1862, Doubleday held the temporary rank of brigadier general. He commanded a brigade at the Second Battle of Bull Run and was a division commander at the Battles of Antietam and Fredericksburg. Promoted to major general, he temporarily led the First Corps at the Battle of Gettysburg in July, 1863. He then was assigned to administrative duties in Washington, D.C. Stationed in San Francisco in 1869, Doubleday acquired the charter of the first cable-operated streetcar line. After retiring from the army in 1873, Doubleday published two volumes of military memoirs. He lived in Mendham, New Jersey, until his death and is buried in Arlington National Cemetery. The Baseball Hall of Fame is situated in Cooperstown, New York, where Doubleday went to school.

E

ELY, Richard Theodore (1854–1943). A political economist, Ely was an influential educator who favored the development of labor unions and public control of natural resources. After graduating from Columbia in 1876, Ely studied in Europe. He was a professor of economics at Johns Hopkins University from 1881 to 1892. That year he became head of the economics department at the University of Wisconsin, a post he held until 1925. He later was a research professor at Northwestern University (1925–1933). Ely helped found the American Economic Association in 1885 and the Institute for Economic Research in 1920. As a founder and editor of the *Journal of Land and Public Utility Economics,* he promoted public control of resources. From 1907 to 1908, he served as the first president of the American Association for Labor Legislation. He supported legislation prohibiting child labor and encouraged the development of labor unions. In 1889, he published *Outlines of Economics,* which became a standard textbook. His other books include *Monopolies and Trusts* (1900), *Foundations of National Prosperity* (1917), and an autobiography, *Ground Under Our Feet* (1938).

F

FIELD, Cyrus West (1819–1892). Field promoted the laying of the Atlantic cable, which permitted instant communication be-

Cyrus Field

tween the United States and Great Britain. Born in Massachusetts, Field left home when he was 15 to work in New York. By 1841, Field had established his own wholesale paper company and nine years later retired with a fortune of $250,000. In 1854, he conceived the possibility of laying a cable on the floor of the Atlantic Ocean between Ireland and Newfoundland. He wrote to Samuel F. B. Morse (1791–1872), the inventor of the telegraph, and Matthew F. Maury (1806–1873), a pioneer in oceanography, to confirm the feasibility of such a project. With their support, Field got a government charter granting him exclusive rights for 50 years. He also secured promises of money and ships from both the British and American governments and $1,500,000 from New York investors. Maury surveyed the route, and in 1857 several hundred miles of cable were laid from Ireland before the cable broke. The Panic of 1857 tied up funds for the rest of the year. In 1858, three unsuccessful attempts were made with British and American ships that met at a midpoint in the ocean to splice the cable ends before heading in opposite directions to lay the cable on the ocean bed. The fourth attempt achieved success on August 5, 1858. Queen **Victoria** (*see*) transmitted the first message to President James Buchanan (1791–1868). Field was acclaimed as a hero. However, when the cable stopped working three weeks later for an unknown reason, Field was accused of faking the cable messages to jump the price of his stock. Field persevered, maintaining contact with influential government leaders all during the Civil War. In 1865, a new attempt was made, using the largest steamship afloat, the *Great Eastern*. The cable broke 1,200 miles from Ireland, but the following year the task was successfully completed. The United States and Britain were united by 2,350 miles of cable. Field later helped finance a system of elevated trains in New York and developed the Wabash Railroad with Jay Gould (1836–1892).

FISKE, John (1842–1901). As a philosopher, historian, and lecturer, Fiske helped to popularize the theory of Social Darwinism in America. Born in Connecticut, Fiske was a child prodigy who had read 200 books by the time he was eight and had a reading knowledge of at least 12 languages before he was 20. Entering Harvard in 1860, he read the works of Herbert Spencer (1820–1903), an English social theorist who had applied the scientific "survival of the fittest" theory of evolution of Charles Darwin (1809–1882) to all fields of human endeavor. Fiske adopted Spencer's viewpoint and in 1862 published an article to that effect

in the *North American Review*. He was threatened with expulsion for his "radical" views but was permitted to graduate in 1863. Without formal study, Fiske passed the bar examinations and became a lawyer in 1865. He started a practice in Boston, but it was unsuccessful. He then lectured on philosophy in Boston and at Harvard until 1872, when he became assistant librarian at Harvard, a post he held for seven years. With the publication of his two-volume *The Outlines of Cosmic Philosophy* in 1874, Fiske became America's foremost exponent of evolution. In an attempt to settle the controversy between science and religion, he contended that evolution was the slow and subtle process by which God makes things come to pass. Fiske concentrated next on numerous volumes of American history, published between 1888 and 1904. Once again applying Spencer's theories, he concluded that Americans, being the descendants of Anglo-Saxons, were the fittest of the human species and America as a nation was destined to excel. Fiske was neither a profound scholar nor an original thinker. He never achieved the professorship he coveted at Harvard, initially because of his radical views on evolution and later because he was judged a mediocre historian. Rather, he was a brilliant intellectual middleman, defending evolution in a charming and lucid manner. From 1879 until his death, he was the most popular—not to mention, at 300 pounds, the largest—American-history lecturer in the nation.

FREEMAN, Mary Eleanor Wilkins (1852–1930). A prolific novelist and writer of short stories, Mrs. Freeman depicted life in ru-

ral New England. She was born in Massachusetts and because of poor health had little formal education. All the members of her family were dead by 1883, and in order to earn a living she began submitting stories to magazines. Her popularity was almost immediate, and her first two collections of short stories, *A Humble Romance* (1887) and *A New England Nun* (1891), are considered her best. Mrs. Freeman, who wrote under her maiden name until her marriage at the age of 50 to Dr. Charles M. Freeman, was the author of 12 novels, including *Pembroke* (1894), and a play dealing with the Salem witchcraft frenzy, *Giles Corey, Yeoman* (1893). However, critics believed that her talents were best suited to short stories. She realistically portrayed the starkness of New England village life in simple, clipped sentences. Mrs. Freeman, **Edith Wharton,** and **Sarah Orne Jewett** (*see both*) were among the last of the genre writers of their time in New England. Upon being married in 1902, Mrs. Freeman moved to Metuchen, New Jersey, where she lived until her death. She published a collection of tales of the supernatural, *The Wind in the Rose Bush*, in 1903 but otherwise wrote very little after her marriage and was largely forgotten by the American reading public. In 1925, however, the American Academy of Arts and Letters awarded her a medal for fiction named in honor of **William Dean Howells** (*see*), and in 1926 she was elected a member of the National Institute of Arts and Letters.

FRENCH, Daniel Chester (1850–1931). A leading American sculptor, French is best remembered for his monumental figure of Abraham Lincoln (1809–1865) inside the Lincoln Memorial in Washington, D. C. Born in New Hampshire, French grew up in Cambridge, Massachusetts. Encouraged by his parents, he learned the rudiments of sculpture and studied drawing at the Massachusetts Institute of Technology. Later, he went to Florence, Italy, to continue his study of sculpture. Receiving his first commission in 1873, French was assigned to design a statue commemorating the centennial of the first battle of the American Revolution. On April 19, 1875, his completed *Minute Man of Concord,* depicting a youth with a plow and a musket, was unveiled before 10,000 spectators, including President Ulysses S. Grant (1822–1885), in Concord,

Sculptor French's Minute Man

Massachusetts. The *Minute Man* established French's reputation and came to symbolize national liberty. Later, during World War I, an engraving of the statue appeared on the nation's war bonds. French's prolific output included a bust of Ralph Waldo Emerson (1803–

1882), modeled from life in 1879, and a bronze statue of John Harvard (1607–1638), completed in 1884, both of which are at Harvard University. *The Republic,* a 24-foot gilded bronze version of a 75-foot-high statue that he created for the World's Columbian Exposition in 1893, now stands in Chicago. French served as a member of the National Commission of Fine Arts, which was established by Congress in 1900 to restore and beautify the nation's capital. In 1912, he became its chairman and that same year was chosen to execute a statue of Lincoln for the inside of the memorial being designed by Henry Bacon (1866–1924). He worked from 1922 to 1931 on the impressive statue of the seated Lincoln.

G

GARDNER, Isabella Stewart (1840–1924). A wealthy socialite and eccentric, Mrs. Gardner built Fenway Court in Boston to house her magnificent art collection and then willed it to that city to be preserved without change as a public museum (*see pp. 978–988*). Born in New York, she married John Lowell Gardner (?–1898), the heir to a $2,500,000 fortune, in 1860 and settled in Boston. Their only child, a 21-month-old son, died in 1865, and thereafter Mrs. Gardner devoted her energies to art and social affairs. Influenced by Harvard art professor Charles Eliot Norton (1827–1908) and Japanese art expert Edward S. Morse (1838–1925), Mrs. Gardner began to collect important works of art. Bernard Berenson (1865–1959), a young art critic, assisted her in making truly unique selections. Mrs. Gardner bought the land for her museum the year fol-

lowing her husband's death and spent the next four years supervising its construction. The museum was her home until her own death and became a salon for gatherings of painters, writers, musicians, and other celebrities. Mrs. Gardner often chose to ignore official Boston society, and among her friends was the prizefighter **John L. Sullivan** (*see*).

GARLAND, Hamlin (1860–1940). Garland is best known for his realistic short stories and novels dealing with farm and prairie life in the latter half of the 19th century. He was raised on small farms in the Midwest, and after being rejected by Harvard, educated himself by reading the works of American and foreign authors and philosophers at the Boston Public Library. His first collection of short stories, *Main-Travelled Roads* (1891), which described the somber realities of life in the Midwest, won him critical, but not popular, acclaim. In 1892, Garland published three novels and one novelette, urging reforms to alleviate various social injustices. He next published a series of essays, *Crumbling Idols* (1894), which established his literary philosophy. Garland emphasized the need for accurate observation and urged artists to record the unpleasant, as well as the pleasant, aspects of life. *Rose of Dutcher's Coolly* (1895), the story of a farm girl's attempts to overcome life's drudgery, is considered by some critics to be his best work. Garland devoted the next 12 years to writing romanticized novels about Indians and the West that were very popular with the public. In 1917, he published the first of a four-volume autobiographical narrative of frontier life, *A Son of the Middle Border.* A sequel, *A Daughter of the Middle Border* (1921), which was about the early years of his marriage to Zulime Taft, won him the Pulitzer Prize for autobiography in 1922. In his later years, Garland published two books dealing with spiritualism, *Forty Years of Psychic Research* (1936) and *The Mystery of the Burned Crosses* (1939).

H

HARRIS, Joel Chandler (1848–1908). The author of the "Uncle Remus" stories, Harris was one of the most popular writers of Southern black folklore and humor in the late 19th and early 20th centuries. Born in Putnam County, Georgia, Harris spent most of his life in his native state. At 13, he became a printer's devil on a weekly newspaper published on a Georgia plantation, where he absorbed the folk tales of the plantation blacks and learned to reproduce their dialect with great precision. After working on newspapers in New Orleans and in several Georgia towns, Harris became a journalist for the Atlanta *Constitution* in 1876. He remained with that paper for 24 years. In the late 1870s, after reading a magazine article on Southern folklore, Harris began publishing in the *Constitution* humorous animal stories for children, drawing on his firsthand knowledge of plantation life and legends. His most successful tales were those in which Uncle Remus, a kindly but shrewd former slave, related to a small boy the adventures of Br'er Rabbit, Br'er Fox, and other members of the plantation menagerie. Harris' first collection of the tales, *Uncle Remus: His Songs and His Sayings,* appeared in 1881 and was followed over the next several decades by

many other Uncle Remus volumes, as well as two adult novels and numerous short stories depicting life in the South. Harris began publishing *Uncle Remus's Magazine* in 1907, the year before his death.

HARTE, Bret (1836–1902). Best known for his colorful stories about life in California, Harte pioneered in the writing of romantic stories about the people and the places that made up the American West. Born in upstate New York, Harte moved to California in 1854. For the next six years, he held various odd jobs,

·VANITY FAIR, JANUARY 4, 1879

Bret Harte

including a position on the staff of the *Northern Californian,* a weekly newspaper. His writings during this period were published in the *Golden Era,* a San Francisco magazine. Harte settled in that city in 1860. He was first hired as a typesetter by the *Era,* and within the next three years he contributed more than 100 sketches and poems to that journal. In 1861, he obtained a

clerkship in the surveyor general's office and later transferred to the Branch Mint. During the mid-1860s, his writings often appeared in the *Californian.* In 1865, Harte published an anthology of California verse under the title *Outcroppings.* Two years later, his first book of poems, *The Lost Galleon and Other Tales,* appeared. In 1868, Harte became the editor of a new magazine, the *Overland Monthly.* In it, he published a short story, "The Luck of Roaring Camp," which signaled his arrival as an author. It was followed by a second story, "The Outcasts of Poker Flat" (1869), which firmly established Harte as a writer of Western local color. His choice of commonplace scenes, his use of regional dialects, and his presentation of character types pioneered a new genre of local-color stories. His comic ballad, "Plain Language from Truthful James," better known as "The Heathen Chinee," was published in 1870 and brought Harte recognition as a humorist in Western dialect. With the publication in Boston of a collection of his works under the title *The Luck of Roaring Camp and Other Sketches* in 1870, he became nationally known. The following year, Harte returned to New York City and signed a $10,000 contract with the *Atlantic Monthly* for one year's work. The quality of his writing, however, was disappointing. To bolster his failing income, Harte went on lecture tours after 1872 and then accepted a post in Germany as a United States consul (1878–1880). He next served (1880–1885) as a consul in Glasgow, Scotland, and afterward moved to London. There, Bret Harte's stories sold well, but he had become little more than a hack writer, turning out new versions of his old California tales. Wearied and ill, he died in London a poor man.

HEARST, George (1820–1891). Starting as a prospector, Hearst made a fortune in mining and founded a newspaper dynasty that still exists today. Hearst left his native Missouri in 1850, and walking beside an ox-drawn wagon, he crossed the Great Plains to California. There, he began the mining of quartz, without success. He then tried his hand at placer mining but again failed. When the Comstock Lode of Nevada was discovered in 1859, Hearst learned that the ore contained silver, which the miners were throwing away, saving only the gold. With $3,500 he had borrowed, he succeeded in purchasing a share of the original claim. The wealth he subsequently acquired laid the foundation for his later fortune. He gradually developed holdings in other mines and became a multimillionaire. Among his most celebrated mines were the Ophir in Nevada, the Anaconda in Montana, the Ontario in Utah, and the Homestake in South Dakota. The last mine, still in existence today, has produced more than $300,000,000 in gold. Hearst's interests also spread into Mexico, where his San Luis mine was situated. In 1880, he purchased the San Francisco *Daily Examiner,* hoping to further his political ambitions. A Democrat, he was defeated for the Senate in 1885 by Leland Stanford (1824–1893). However, in 1886 Hearst was appointed to the United States Senate to finish an unexpired term. Two years later, he was elected for a full term. His interests in the Senate paralleled those of his business life—mining, agriculture, and railroads. His wife, Phoebe Apperson

Hearst (1842–1919), was a noted philanthropist. His son, William Randolph Hearst (1863–1951), later expanded the family's newspaper interests into an empire of 25 newspapers, a wire service, and three radio stations.

HOAR, George (1826–1904). As a Representative and Senator from Massachusetts, Hoar earned a reputation as an uncompromising idealist in an age marked by political corruption. He graduated from Harvard in 1846 and from Harvard Law School three years later. He then opened a law practice and helped to organize the Republican Party. After terms in both houses of the state legislature, he was elected to Congress in 1869 and served four successive terms in the House. In 1877, Hoar was elected to the Senate, where he served until his death. During his 35 years on Capitol Hill, Hoar sought justice for blacks and Indians, opposed American acquisition of Cuba and the Philippines, fought against religious intolerance, and supported the direct election of Senators. A year before his death, Hoar summed up his philosophy, saying "If my life has been worth anything, it has been because I have insisted, to the best of my ability, that these three things—love of God, love of country, and manhood—are the essential and fundamental things, and that race, color, and creed are unessential and accidental." Hoar spent much of his time promoting scholarship and was instrumental in the founding of Worcester Polytechnic Institute and Clark University in Worcester, Massachusetts. He also served as president of both the American Historical Association and the American Antiquarian Society and as a regent of the Smithsonian Institution.

HOLMES, Oliver Wendell (1841–1935). This Supreme Court Justice, known as the Great Dissenter, possessed an insight into the nature of the legal process unsurpassed by any other jurist. As a result, he exerted a powerful in-

NEW YORK PUBLIC LIBRARY

Oliver Wendell Holmes

fluence upon subsequent generations of lawyers and judges. Born into a distinguished Boston family—his father, Oliver Wendell Holmes (1809–1894), was a famous author—Holmes grew up in an atmosphere where wit and intellect were cultivated. Following his graduation from Harvard in 1861, he served in the Union Army and was wounded three times. After his discharge in 1864, he enrolled at Harvard Law School, from which he received a degree in 1866. Holmes practiced law in Boston, taught briefly at Harvard, and also edited the *American Law Review* from 1870 to 1873. In a treatise, published in 1881 and entitled *The Common Law,* Holmes expressed the legal philosophy that later shaped his future decisions as a judge. The law, he said, is not simply a body of settled doctrine handed down

Winslow Homer portrayed Maine fishermen at work in The Herring Net.

from the past, but rather a living organism capable of being adapted to the needs of a rapidly changing society. As he put it, "The life of the law has not been logic: it has been experience." This treatise was immediately acclaimed, and Holmes was made a professor at Harvard Law School, where he taught until he was appointed to the Massachusetts supreme court in 1882. Serving there for 20 years, Holmes wrote nearly 1,300 opinions. He occasionally dissented from the majority by defending the rights of labor, and he came to be regarded as a "dangerous" radical by some of his more conservative colleagues. However, his liberal views won the admiration of President Theodore Roosevelt (1858–1919), who named Holmes to the United States Supreme Court in 1902. During his 29 years as an Associate Justice, Holmes often dissented from the rest of the Court by consistently defending human rights, which he felt were necessary to the functioning of a free society. He voiced his concern for free speech in *Schenk vs. the United States,* a case in which the Court unanimously upheld the Espionage Act passed by Congress in World War I. Holmes, agreeing that the defendant was guilty, took the occasion to enunciate the doctrine of "clear and present danger." He argued that although no one has the right to falsely cry *fire* in a crowded theater, the mere presence of an untruth in a speech is not enough to convict a man. Therefore, he concluded, Congressional interference with freedom of speech is not justified, except in times of national danger. Holmes adamantly believed that "The best test of truth is the power of the thought to get itself accepted in the competition of

the market." A widower, Holmes retired from the bench in 1932, and upon his death three years later, left the bulk of his estate to the United States government.

HOMER, Winslow (1836–1910). Best known for his dramatic seascapes, Homer was an artist with a uniquely American style of painting. Born and raised in the vicinity of Boston, Homer was apprenticed to a lithographer in 1855. He designed title pages for sheet music and sketched members of the state senate. Primarily a self-taught artist, he opened his own Boston studio in 1857 and began illustrating popular magazines of the period, and two years later he moved to New York City. In 1861, *Harper's Weekly* employed Homer to attend and sketch the inaugural of President-elect Abraham Lincoln (1809–1865). During the Civil War, *Harper's* sent Homer as an artist-correspondent to the battlefront, where he depicted some early engagements and sketched the everyday lives of Union soldiers camped in Virginia. Back in New York, Homer converted his war sketches into oil paintings (*see pp. 712 and 715*), exhibited them at the National Gallery in Washington, D.C., (1863–1866), and won international acclaim. After spending 10 months in Paris in 1867, Homer returned to the United States and devoted himself mainly to portraying peculiarly American subjects, as well

as more conventional scenes (*see p. 971*). In the late 1860s, he was among the first of his countrymen to depict blacks in several realistic studies. A trip to an English fishing village in 1881 inspired Homer to paint seascapes. He settled in Prout's Neck, Maine, and spent the last three decades of his life painting marine masterpieces in oils and watercolors.

HOWELLS, William Dean (1837–1920). Sometimes called the dean of America's men of letters, this novelist based his writings on the actual and observable, rather than on the romantic. He believed that art should have a moral purpose and should teach rather than amuse. He thus influenced the development of the American school of realistic fiction. Howells was born in Ohio. He received little formal education and from the age of nine worked as a typesetter in his father's printing shop. Settling in Columbus in 1856, Howells worked there five years as a newspaper reporter for the *Ohio State Journal*. After publishing a successful campaign biography of Abraham Lincoln (1809–1865) in 1860, Howells was appointed United States consul to Venice in 1861. Upon his return to America four years later, he moved to Cambridge, Massachusetts. There, he became an assistant editor of the *Atlantic Monthly* and served as its editor in chief from 1871 to 1881. During this period, Howells wrote several novels, most of which were spoofs of American manners. The first to be published was *Their Wedding Journey* (1872). After 1881, Howells abandoned this type of writing in favor of realistic character studies. His masterpiece, *The Rise of Silas Lapham,* a story of a self-made man from Boston, was published in 1885. That same year, Howells became a contributor to *Harper's Magazine,* on which he worked until 1891, when he moved to New York. He then turned to the social, economic, and religious problems created by an industrial society in his realistic fiction. By the turn of the century, Howells was considered by many to be the nation's leading author and for the rest of his life was a major influence on such realists as **Hamlin Garland, Frank Norris,** and **Stephen Crane** (*see all*). From 1908 until his death, Howells served as the first president of the American Academy of Arts and Letters. One of the most prolific writers of his day, Howells wrote about 35 novels, four books of poetry, more than 30 volumes of essays, six volumes of criticism, and more than 30 plays, as well as several autobiographical sketches and travel accounts.

HULL HOUSE. *See* **Addams, Jane.**

HUNT, Richard Morris (1827–1895). A noted American architect, Hunt is most famous for the ornate and ostentatious mansions that he built for millionaires in New York City and Newport, Rhode Island, in the last quarter of the 19th century. His designs followed several different historical styles, notably that of the French Renaissance. Born in Brattleboro, Vermont, Hunt lived abroad from 1843 to 1855. He studied architecture in Geneva, Switzerland, and traveled throughout Europe as well as in Asia Minor and Egypt. However, he spent most of his time in Paris, where, among other things, he was the first American to study architecture at the Ecole des Beaux-Arts. Hunt's first job after his return to the United States was as assistant to Thomas U. Walter (1804–1887) in the construction of the dome that was then being added to the Capitol in Washington, D. C. In the winter of 1856–1857, Hunt settled in New York, where in 1858 he established the first studio in America for the teaching of architecture. Following a stay of several years in Europe, he returned to America and designed the New York Tribune Building. Built in 1873–1874, it was the first elevator office building in the United States. Hunt also designed the pedestal for the Statue of Liberty in New York Harbor. He first gained national acclaim in 1878 when he began building the famous New York town house for the railroad magnate William Kissam Vanderbilt (1849–1920). Situated on the northwest corner of Fifth Avenue and 52nd Street, it was a château in the style of the French Renaissance (*see p. 906*). Hunt's two other important New York mansions, also on Fifth Avenue, were built for Elbridge T. Gerry (1837–1927) and John Jacob Astor (1864–1912). All of them have since been demolished. Hunt also constructed Biltmore, a palatial French Renaissance mansion outside the city of Asheville, North Carolina, for George W. Vanderbilt (1862–1914). It is now a museum. Hunt's many successful Newport residences include Ochre Court, a late Gothic French château that now houses Salva Regina College, and Belcourt, a Gothic palace built for Oliver H. P. Belmont (1858–1908) that is now a museum. Hunt also remodeled The Breakers, Newport's most celebrated mansion, for Cornelius Vanderbilt (1843–1899). It too is now a museum. Hunt helped found the American Institute of Architects in 1857 and served variously as its secretary (1857–1860) and president (1888–1891). His brother, William Morris Hunt (1824–1879), was a famous painter.

I

INGERSOLL, Robert Green (1833–1899). Known to his contemporaries as the Great Agnostic, Ingersoll used his considerable skill as an orator to attack orthodox Christianity. Born in upstate New York, Ingersoll was the son of a minister but never accepted traditional religious beliefs. Living in Ohio, Wisconsin, and Illinois as a youth, Ingersoll received little formal schooling. However, he became a lawyer and was ad-

Robert G. Ingersoll

mitted to the Illinois bar in 1855. He then practiced law in Peoria and ran unsuccessfully as a Democrat for Congress in 1860. An abolitionist, Ingersoll broke with the Democrats in 1861 over the slavery issue and served as a colonel in the Union Army during the Civil War. Afterward, he joined the Republican Party and was elected attorney general (1867–1869) of Illinois. Many historians believe that he could have become that state's governor but for his skeptical attitude about the existence of God. Ingersoll believed that a man could lead a moral life without being religious. While serving as a delegate to the Republican National Convention in Cincinnati in 1876, Ingersoll nominated James G. Blaine (1830–1893), describing the Presidential candidate as a "plumed knight." Although Blaine lost the nomination, Ingersoll achieved nationwide fame, and for the next 20 years he received as much as $3,500 each for lectures. He spoke before audiences of unprecedented size, defending his agnostic views. Devout Americans regarded him as a heathen. However, millions of people supported Ingersoll's efforts to end the bigotry and superstition that he believed organized religion fostered. Meanwhile, he continued his law practice and in 1879 moved to Washington, D. C. His greatest legal victory occurred in 1882–1883 when he successfully defended the Republican politicians involved in a government mail fraud known as the Star Route Scandal. After campaigning for the gold standard in the elections of 1896, Ingersoll retired from public life.

IVES, James Merritt. *See* **Currier and Ives.**

J

JAMES, Henry (1843–1916). One of the foremost contributors to the development of the modern novel, James pioneered in the technique of psychological realism and mastered a highly structured prose style considered unexcelled for its subtle

Henry James

phrases and rhythms. James was born in New York City into a wealthy, cosmopolitan family. His older brother, **William James** (*see*), became a noted philosopher. Henry James was educated by private tutors until 1855, when his parents took him to live in Europe for three years. Unable to serve in the Union Army during the Civil War because of a back ailment, Henry briefly attended Harvard Law School in 1862 and became acquainted in Cambridge with **William Dean Howells, James Russell Lowell,** and **Charles Eliot Norton** (*see all*). They encouraged him to become a writer. From 1865 to 1869, James contributed critical articles and short stories to such literary magazines as the *Nation,*

Atlantic Monthly, and *Galaxy.* During this time, he also traveled back and forth between Europe and Cambridge, Massachusetts, and began to think of himself as a detached observer of life. He came to believe that America stifled creative talent and offered little subject matter. In 1875, James moved to Paris, where he met Guy de Maupassant (1850–1893), Gustave Flaubert (1821–1880), and Ivan Turgenev (1818–1883). The following year, he made London his permanent residence. A prolific writer, James in his lifetime published 19 novels, about 100 short stories, three volumes of plays, and numerous biographical, autobiographical, and critical pieces. His themes often dealt with expatriated Americans. His first influential novel, *The Portrait of a Lady* (1881), was a study of the reactions of an innocent American girl who is confronted with the complexities and sophistication of European civilization. In his later works of fiction, James concentrated on the technique of writing. *The Wings of the Dove* (1902), *The Ambassadors* (1903), and *The Golden Bowl* (1904) are thought by critics to be his greatest works. James himself believed *The Ambassadors* to be the most perfectly constructed of his novels. At the outbreak of World War I, James became a British subject, but upon his death in 1916 his ashes were sent back to Cambridge for burial. James' work was not fully appreciated until his death. The poet T. S. Eliot (1888–1965) once said, "No novelist in our language can approach Henry James."

JAMES, William (1842–1910). A philosopher and psychologist, James was one of the founders of the philosophy of pragmatism and did much to establish psychology as an independent science. Born into a cosmopolitan New York family that included his brother, novelist **Henry James** (*see*), William was educated by private tutors before going abroad for further education. He obtained his medical degree from Harvard in 1869 and joined the Harvard faculty as an instructor in physiology three years later. He taught at Harvard in various departments until his retirement in 1907. In 1875, James initiated a course called Relations between Physiology and Psychology, which the next year led to the opening of the first psychology laboratory in America. In 1890, he published *The Principles of Psychology,* which, in an abridged form, became the standard text for psychology courses. In one of its chapters, James advanced the idea of the stream of consciousness, which later became an important technique in fiction. Unlike the Social Darwinists of his day (*see* **John Fiske**), James believed that an individual could exercise free will in determining his own fate. He contended that the test of a truth should be the conduct it inspires. If an idea has no consequences, it has no meaning. His book expounding this philosophy, *Pragmatism,* was published in 1907. Critics labeled his philosophy as vulgar expediency and accused James of thinking that anything that works is good. He replied to his critics in *The Meaning of Truth* (1909). One of James' notable converts to pragmatism was educator **John Dewey** (*see*). James' revolt against absolutes extended to religion. In 1902, he published *The Varieties of Religious Experience,* which contended that any article of religious faith was "true" if it gave emotional satisfaction. James contin-

William James

ued writing until a month before his death and was recognized as one of the most important American philosophers in the nation's history.

JENNEY, William (1832–1907). Jenney was the architect who designed the first skyscraper in America. The Massachusetts-born designer studied architecture at the Lawrence Scientific School of Harvard University and later at the Ecole Centrale des Arts et Manufactures in Paris. At the beginning of the Civil War, he enlisted in the Union Army. He was assigned to the staff of General William T. Sherman (1820–1891) and subsequently became chief engineer of the Fifteenth Army Corps. After the war, he settled in Chicago, where he established himself as an engineer and architect. In 1883, Jenney constructed the Home Insurance Building in that city. To erect the building, he designed a system of skeleton construction in which each story was independently supported on columns. Because it was the first high building to employ skeleton construction as the basic principle of its design, it

is considered the first skyscraper. Although the columns were made largely of cast iron, Jenney introduced the use of Bessemer steel beams in the building. In 1891, he formed an architectural firm that later became Jenney, Mundie & Jensen. Jenney's other works in Chicago include the Siegel Cooper & Company store, the YMCA, the Chicago National Bank, and the Horticulture Building at the World's Columbian Exposition of 1893. Jenney retired to Los Angeles in 1905.

JEWETT, Sarah Orne (1849–1909). A popular author, Miss Jewett excelled in her sketches and stories of New England life. As a child in South Berwick, Maine, she developed a keen awareness of the people and the area through numerous trips with her father, a doctor, on his rounds. She had little formal education but read widely. At 14, she was particularly influenced by *The Pearl of Orr's Island* (1862), by Harriet Beecher Stowe (1811–1896), a book that sympathetically depicted the vanishing port towns of the Maine coast. Miss Jewett decided to try herself to capture in words the diminishing grandeur of Maine's countryside and harbors. The *Atlantic Monthly* accepted one of her early stories, "Mr. Bruce," which she wrote when she was 19. In 1873, the magazine also printed "The Shore House," a sketch that so much impressed its editor, **William Dean Howells** (*see*), that he convinced Miss Jewett to publish it as a book, with a series of vignettes written about a village she called Deephaven. *Deephaven* was published in 1877. This collection established Miss Jewett as one of New England's leading writers. In 1896, she published what is considered her finest work, *The Country of the Pointed Firs,* a group of sketches about a declining Maine seaport in the era after the West Indies trading days. After her father died in 1878, Miss Jewett began a close, lifelong friendship with Annie Adams Fields (1834–1915), wife of the publisher James Fields (1817–1881). Although she was a frequent visitor to Mrs. Fields' literary salon in Boston and made several trips abroad, Miss Jewett always returned to her native town in Maine for long periods of work. During her later years, she turned to writing historical romance and children's books.

L

LONGFELLOW, Henry Wadsworth (1807–1882). During his lifetime, Longfellow was the most famous and popular poet in the United States, and when he died, he was the first American to be honored in the Poet's Corner of London's Westminster Abbey. Born in Portland, Maine, Longfellow graduated from Bowdoin College in 1825. He subsequently traveled in Europe before teaching modern languages, first at Bowdoin (1829–1835) and then at Harvard (1836–1854). An outstanding linguist, he knew Finnish and Icelandic as well as the major European languages. His translations—from 11 different foreign tongues—include *The Divine Comedy of Dante Alighieri* (1867). Longfellow published two prose compositions—*Outre-Mer: A Pilgrimage Beyond the Sea* (1833–1834) and *Hyperion* (1839)—before compiling his first volume of poetry, *Voices of the Night,* in 1839. He then published *Ballads and Other Poems* (1842), which contains some of his most famous poems, including "The Village Blacksmith," "The Wreck of the Hesperus," and "Excelsior." Longfellow was a prolific writer, and among his most popular works are three long historical narrative poems, *Evangeline* (1847), *The Song of Hiawatha* (1855), and *The Courtship of Miles Standish* (1858). In 1860, he published *Birds of Passage,* which contains "The Children's Hour," a well-known poem about his three daughters. The following year, he published one of his most acclaimed narrative poems, "Paul Revere's Ride," which later was included in *The Tales of a Wayside Inn* (1863). Because of his sentimentality and moralizing, Longfellow's popularity declined in the 20th century. Nevertheless, he still holds a significant position in America's literary heritage.

LOWELL, James Russell (1819–1891). As a poet, editor, critic, and diplomat, Lowell was among the foremost men of letters of his time and exerted a great influence on the formation of public opinion and taste. Born in Cambridge, Massachusetts, and descended from a prominent colonial family, Lowell graduated from Harvard in 1838 and received a law degree two years later. He did not practice law, however, but began writing poetry instead. Under the influence of his future wife, Maria White (1821–1853), an ardent abolitionist, he published in 1844 *Poems,* a volume containing several antislavery themes. By the time he was 29, Lowell had established himself as a versatile, competent author and had won public acclaim for his second book of *Poems,* a long parable in verse entitled "The Vision of Sir Launfal," the humorous essay

James Russell Lowell

"A Fable for Critics," and the first of two series of *The Biglow Papers,* a political satire. In the last, Lowell criticized the nation's conduct of the Mexican War through the character of a rustic Yankee clergyman. In 1855, Lowell succeeded **Henry Wadsworth Longfellow** (*see*) as professor of Spanish and French at Harvard and taught there for 31 years. While there, Lowell devoted himself more and more to the scholarly pursuit of literary criticism. He served as the first editor of the liberal magazine *Atlantic Monthly* from 1857 to 1861. During the Civil War, he wrote his second series of *The Biglow Papers*—this time a criticism of British involvement in the war—for the *Atlantic Monthly.* Both series are considered by some critics as Lowell's most important literary contribution. One of his best poems, "Ode Recited at the Harvard Commemoration," was written in 1865 in honor of the students who had lost their lives in the war. From 1864 to 1872, Lowell was associate editor of the *North American Review,* and he used it to express his views on politics and contemporary writing. As a Presidential elector in 1876, Lowell supported Rutherford B.

Hayes (1822–1893) and was rewarded with the diplomatic post of minister to Spain (1877–1880). After subsequently serving as minister to Britain (1880–1885), Lowell retired from public life.

M

MOODY, Dwight Lyman (1837–1899). Moody was the most successful evangelistic preacher in America during the 19th century. A Protestant layman, he had no formal church organization to back his missionary work. However, combining business and promotional ability with a zeal for spreading the Christian gospel, he carried his conversion crusades to millions in the United States and Great Britain between 1860 and 1899. Moody was born in Northfield, Massachusetts. He left school at the age of 13 to work, first as a farm laborer, and then as a clerk in his uncle's shoe store in Boston. In 1856, he moved to Chicago, where he became a prosperous wholesale shoe salesman. He left business in 1860 to devote himself full-time to missionary work in cities. Moody's personal evangelism dealt in neither abstract theology nor faith healing. The popularity of his "old-time religion" was due to the simple and direct way that he conveyed the message of Christian salvation. He emphasized God's fatherly love, rather than the punishment of hellfire and damnation. Moody was instrumental in promoting the spread of Young Men's Christian Associations to college campuses throughout the nation. During the Civil War, he ministered frequently to wounded soldiers. For many years, Moody was associated with the organist and gospel singer Ira D. Sankey (1840–1908), with whom he compiled a hymnbook of immense popularity. The Moody-Sankey mass revivals in England, Scotland, and Ireland (1873–1875 and 1881–1883) gained them international recognition. Profits from their tours and sales of the hymnal were used by Moody for philanthropic purposes. He founded Northfield Seminary for girls in 1879, Mount Hermon School for boys

Dwight Lyman Moody

in 1881, and the Chicago Bible Institute (now the Moody Bible Institute) in 1889. Eighteen volumes of Moody's sermons were compiled during his lifetime.

N

NATION, Carrie Amelia Moore (1846–1911). This hatchet-wielding woman earned nationwide notoriety for her vigorous campaign against liquor and saloons in the early 1900s. Born in Garrard County, Kentucky, Carrie may have inherited her turbulent personality from her mentally ill mother. She settled in Missouri, where she married Dr. Charles Gloyd, an alcoholic, in 1867. Failing to reform her husband, Carrie deserted him and henceforth denounced the evils of intoxicating spirits. She became a teacher and then married a one-time lawyer and minister, David Nation, in 1877. Twelve years later, the couple moved to Medicine Lodge, Kansas. Although Kansas had prohibited the sale of liquor in 1880, it still had "joints" that openly sold alcoholic beverages. To combat this, Carrie organized a branch of the **Woman's Christian Temperance Union** (*see*) about 1890 and vociferously fought the "jointists" throughout the next decade. Acting upon the premise that because saloons were illegal she could destroy saloon property with impunity, Carrie, in 1900, armed herself with a hatchet and began wrecking the saloons in Wichita. As a result, she was jailed for seven weeks, but upon her release she continued her "hatchetations" in other parts of Kansas and in such cities as New York, Washington, D. C., and San Francisco. Carrie was arrested about 30 times and was often threatened with physical harm by angry saloonkeepers. She raised the money to pay the fines levied against her by delivering lectures, making stage appearances, and selling miniature silver hatchets as souvenirs. Although organized temperance movements disapproved of her methods and gave her little support, Carrie succeeded in mobilizing public opinion to begin a drive for national prohibition, which went into effect in 1920 with the ratification of the Eighteenth Amendment.

NATIONAL WOMAN SUFFRAGE ASSOCIATION. The National Woman Suffrage Association was formed in 1869 to gain women the right to vote. An earlier organization, the Equal Rights Association, had been established after the Civil War to further the interests of both women and blacks. However, the question of enfranchising women became overshadowed by the securing of full rights for former slaves. Two leading reformers, Susan B. Anthony (1820–1906) and Elizabeth Cady Stanton (1815–1902), sought the aid of Horace Greeley (1811–1872), publisher of the New York *Tribune*. However, he put them off, saying, "Your turn will come next. I conjure you to remember that this is the Negro's hour." Despite the rebuff, the women decided to establish a separate organization to promote female suffrage. They organized the National Woman Suffrage Association in 1869. Mrs. Stanton became president and Miss Anthony chairman of the executive committee. Other reformers, however, objected to the association's aim of obtaining a specific suffrage amendment to the United States Constitution. They preferred instead to gain the vote through amendments to state constitutions. These reformers formed another organization, the American Woman Suffrage Association, of which Henry Ward Beecher (1813–1887) became president and Lucy Stone (1818–1893) chairman of the executive committee. The dispute was finally resolved in 1890, when the two organizations decided to pursue both goals together. They combined under the name National American Woman Suffrage Association. Mrs. Stanton was elected president of the new body; Miss Anthony, vice-president-at-large; Miss Stone, chairman of the executive committee. As a result of their ef-

forts, by 1914 almost all of the states in the West allowed women to vote. This was because women had played such a large role in the building of frontier communities. However, in the East, a coalition of corporations, party machines, and liquor interests blocked their path. Corporations feared female support of antitrust, child-labor, and pro-union laws. Party machines feared a disruption of their political control, and the liquor interests were worried that women would support prohibition. However, during World War I, when so many women went to work in factories, New York State amended its constitution to allow women to vote. Other states in the East soon followed suit, and in the spring of 1919 a special session of Congress passed the Nineteenth Amendment, granting women full suffrage in all elections. Twenty-nine states called special sessions of their legislatures and ratified the amendment in time for the national elections of November, 1920, when women throughout the nation first voted for President.

NINETEENTH AMENDMENT. *See* **National Woman Suffrage Association.**

NORRIS, Benjamin Franklin ("Frank") (1870–1902). Frank Norris was a journalist and novelist who realistically described how the forces of an industrial society defeated the ordinary man. Born in Chicago, he enrolled in the University of California in 1890 to study literature. There, he was strongly influenced by the writing of the French author Emile Zola (1840–1902). While still a senior, Norris began *McTeague,* the study of a man's disintegration under

financial pressure. He left the university in 1894 and entered Harvard as a special student in creative writing. He continued to work on *McTeague* and also wrote parts of *Vandover and the Brute,* the story of a man's degradation. In 1895, Norris went to South Africa as a correspondent for the San Francisco *Chronicle.* After his return in 1896, he joined the staff of a small weekly

Frank Norris

magazine, the *Wave.* His novel, *Moran of the Lady Letty,* was serialized in that journal and came to the attention of the editors of *McClure's Magazine.* In 1898, Norris was invited to New York to join its staff and that same year was assigned to Cuba to cover the Spanish-American War. Upon returning, he published *McTeague* and another novel, *Blix,* in 1899. He was then hired by a publishing house to read manuscripts. Norris—a writer who believed in looking at life scientifically, without making idealizations—next planned to write an epic trilogy in which wheat would symbolize the force of nature as it shaped the lives of men. The first novel in the "The Epic of Wheat" was *The Octopus* (1901), a story about the struggle of California wheat growers against the railroads. The second, *The Pit* (1903), described the greed of speculators in Chicago's wheat market. The third novel, *The Wolf*, would have described a starving foreign community. It was unfinished when Norris died of complications following an appendicitis operation at the age of 32.

O

OAKLEY, Annie (1860–1926). Annie was an Ohio farm girl who became world famous as a trick marksman. One of seven children in a destitute family, Phoebe Anne Oakley Mozee began shooting rabbits and squirrels for her family's meals. She was such an excellent shot that by the age of 10 she was shipping surplus game to sell in Cincinnati. Within five years, the youngster's earnings paid off the mortgage on the family farm. When Annie was 15, she attended a shooting exhibition in Cincinnati. The touring marksman, Frank E. Butler (?–1926), challenged anyone in the audience to outshoot him. Annie accepted the challenge and defeated Butler by one point. The two then fell in love and married within a year. Butler subsequently became his wife's business manager. Under his guidance, she became a spectacular exhibition shooter. In 1885, the Butlers joined the Wild West show of **Buffalo Bill Cody** (*see*) and traveled with the troupe until 1902. Annie's fame as a sharpshooter grew with each performance. While riding a horse, she could break glass balls thrown into the air. She could hit the thin edge of a playing card at

BUFFALO BILL'S WILD WEST·
CONGRESS, ROUGH RIDERS OF THE WORLD.

MISS ANNIE OAKLEY,
THE PEERLESS LADY WING-SHOT.

30 paces and shoot pennies from between her husband's fingers. In one of her stunts, she perforated playing cards tossed in the air. Tickets with holes punched in them are still called Annie Oakleys. When Buffalo Bill Cody took his Wild West show to Europe in 1887, Annie became an international celebrity. She was presented to Queen **Victoria** (*see*) and outshot Grand Duke Michael (1832–1909) of Russia. In 1901, Annie was partly paralyzed in a railroad accident. She recovered, however, and in the following two decades set some of her best shooting records.

OCHS, Adolph Simon (1858–1935). Assuming control of the bankrupt New York *Times* in 1896, Ochs transformed it into the most influential newspaper in America. Ochs, who was born in Ohio and raised in Knoxville, Tennessee, joined the staff of the Chattanooga *Dispatch* in 1877, and soon became its editor in chief. The following year, Ochs borrowed $250 and bought controlling interest in the Chattanooga *Times*, which he developed into the state's leading newspaper. Before acquiring the New York *Times*, he also established *The Tradesman*, a busi-

ness periodical, and the Southern Associated Press. Competition from other newspapers during the Spanish-American War in 1898 nearly drove the New York *Times* out of business, but Ochs managed to survive by dropping its price from 3¢ to 1¢. By 1900, after he had added a Sunday book-review section and a Sunday magazine, the *Times* was making a profit. Ochs stressed nonpartisan news reporting and made an effort to eliminate fraudulent advertising. The paper's motto was and still is, "All The News That's Fit To Print." The *Times*' excellent coverage of World War I helped to establish it as the newspaper of historical record in America. In 1924, Ochs donated $500,000 to make possible the publication of the *Dictionary of American Biography*. Ochs was succeeded as publisher of the *Times* by his son-in-law, Arthur Hays Sulzberger (1891–1969), and the newspaper is still controlled by the Sulzberger family.

OLMSTED, Frederick Law (1822–1903). The leading landscape architect of his day, Olmsted designed Central Park in New York City, Yosemite National Park in California, and the Capitol grounds in Washington, D. C., and also prepared the general plan for the landscaping of Niagara Falls. Olmsted studied agriculture and engineering at Yale in 1847 but left to take up farming in his native Connecticut and later on Staten Island. In 1850, he toured Britain and the Continent, recording his travels in a book. In the 1850s, he made three trips to the South. His observations were described in three books later reprinted under a single title, *The Cotton Kingdom* (1861), which is still considered one of the most valuable

Frederick Law Olmsted

accounts of the prewar South. In 1857, Olmsted launched his career as a landscape architect by seeking an appointment as superintendent of Central Park. The city had been persuaded by William Cullen Bryant (1794–1878) of the New York *Evening Post* and other people to create a vast park for public recreational purposes. Ultimately, 840 acres were set aside. Clearing had already begun on the site when a plan submitted by Olmsted and Calvert Vaux (1824–1895), an English architect, was accepted in competition against other designs. Olmsted was appointed chief architect. When he began his work in 1858, the city of New York reached only to 34th Street. The area designated for the park—now stretching from 59th to 110th Streets—was swampy and filled with squatters' shacks, pig farms, and rugged rocks. Using more than 10,000,000 carloads of earth for filler and 4,000,000 trees and shrubs, Olmsted and Vaux created a rustic pleasure land of walks, bridle paths, and carriage ways unencumbered by buildings and

containing 185 acres of lakes and pools (*see p. 920*). The basic work was finished in four years, but the park was not fully completed until 1876. Olmsted worked on and off with the project throughout this period. During the Civil War, he was appointed to head the United States Sanitary Commission (1861–1863), a forerunner of the Red Cross. Moving west, Olmsted worked with the state of California preparing a preservation plan for the Yosemite Forest (now Yosemite National Park) and designed the campus for the University of California at Berkeley in 1865. In all, Olmsted planned more than 80 parks, including Prospect Park in Brooklyn, the Fenway in Boston, Belle Isle in Detroit, and Mount Royal Park in Montreal. In 1874, he was called upon to landscape the Capitol grounds in Washington, D. C., and in 1879 to save the Niagara Falls area from deterioration. In 1890, Olmsted was selected by Daniel Burnham (1846–1912) as chief architect of the World's Columbian Exposition of 1893 in Chicago. Praising Olmsted's success in shaping the fairgrounds, Burnham said, "He paints with lakes and wooded slopes; with lawns and banks and forest-covered hills; with mountainsides and ocean views." Much of Olmsted's original design remains today as Jackson Park. Olmsted retired in 1895, having made the public park a fact of life for city dwellers across the nation.

OPTIC, Oliver (1822–1897). Optic was the main rival of **Horatio Alger** (*see*) for the youthful reading audience of his day. He wrote about 120 books and more than 1,000 short stories, most of them adventure yarns for boys. Born William Taylor Adams in Bel-

lingham, Massachusetts, Optic was the son of a tavern keeper and farmer. He acquired a hard-won education and then became a teacher and principal in the Boston public school system (1845–1865). Taking for his pseudonym the name of a character in a play he had seen, he began writing juvenile fiction for periodicals about 1850 and then turned to publishing several series of boys' books. Among them were the *Boat Club* series, which first appeared in 1854, the *Army and Navy* series (1865), the *Onward and Upward* series (1870), and the *Yacht Club* series (1872). Optic's extensive travels in Europe, Asia, and Africa furnished him with ample material for his stories, whose exciting exploits and "character-building" moral messages were eagerly absorbed by more than a million young readers. After retiring from teaching in 1865, Optic edited *Oliver Optic's Magazine for Boys and Girls* and later the periodicals *Our Little Ones* and *Student and Schoolmate*.

P

PAGE, Thomas Nelson (1853–1922). A writer of short stories, novels, and verse, Page specialized in romantic characterizations of the Old South around the time of the Civil War. His family was one of the aristocratic families in Virginia whose fortunes were lost in the war. Page received his law degree in 1874 and opened a practice in Richmond. His verses, written in a Southern dialect, were published as early as 1877. With the publication in 1884 of his first story, "Marse Chan," his reputation was established. In 1887, "Marse Chan," "Meh Lady," and other stories—most of which were written in black dialect—appeared in one volume, *In Ole Virginia*. Page believed that the South had been a paradise before the Civil War, populated by happy slaves and kindly masters. His purpose in writing was to heal the breach between the North and the South by presenting a sympathetic picture of the past. Page's books, which were best sellers in their day, included *Red Rock* (1898), a novel depicting a Southern revolt against Reconstruction. It is credited by some with inspiring a revival of the Ku Klux Klan. Among his other works were a children's book, *Two Little Confederates* (1888); a collection of verses in dialect, *Befo' de War* (1888); and a serious study of the South, *The Negro, The Southerner's Problem* (1904). In 1913, President Woodrow Wilson (1856–1924) appointed Page ambassador to Italy, and he served in that position until 1919. Upon returning to America, he wrote a sympathetic account of Italy's part in World War I, entitled *Italy and the World War* (1920).

PARRINGTON, Vernon Louis (1871–1929). A critic, scholar, and teacher, Parrington was one of America's most influential literary and intellectual historians. His *Main Currents in American Thought,* published in three volumes between 1927 and 1930, traces and interprets—from an economic and political point of view—the development of ideas in American literature from colonial times to 1920. The first two volumes of Parrington's work, *The Colonial Mind* and *The Romantic Revolution in America,* won him the Pulitzer Prize for history in 1928. Born in Illinois, Parrington spent his boyhood in Kansas, where the

prevailing Populist and liberal sentiment shaped much of his thinking. He attended the College of Emporia in Kansas and then studied two years at Harvard, graduating in 1893. He then became a teacher of English and modern languages, first at the College of Emporia (1893–1897), then at the University of Oklahoma (1897–1908), and finally at the University of Washington (1908–1929). Parrington was a brilliant and popular teacher, but he received little attention beyond his classroom until the appearance of the first volume of his masterpiece, *Main Currents*. Parrington wrote with high artistry, wit, and originality, and his well-researched writing reflected his Jeffersonian-type liberalism Among his other published works are *The Connecticut Wits* (1926) and *Sinclair Lewis, Our Own Diogenes* (1927). Parrington died suddenly, while on a visit to England in 1929. The third volume of *Main Currents, The Beginnings of Critical Realism in America,* was published in incomplete form after his death.

PULITZER, Joseph (1847–1911). A famous journalist and newspaper publisher, Pulitzer left a bequest of $2,000,000 to found the Columbia University Graduate School of Journalism in New York City and to finance the Pulitzer Prizes—annual awards in the fields of journalism, history, letters, and music. Pulitzer, who came to America from his native Hungary when he was 17, began working as a reporter in St. Louis for the *Westliche Post,* a German-language newspaper, in 1868. He soon became a respected journalist and the holder of several local political offices. After buying the St. Louis *Dispatch* in 1878, he merged it with the *Post* to form the St. Louis

Joseph Pulitzer

Post-Dispatch. Under his management, the *Post-Dispatch* became an extremely successful paper, and in 1883 Pulitzer was able to purchase the New York *World* from financier Jay Gould (1836–1892). He intended it to be a high-quality journal with extensive news coverage. Pulitzer introduced a number of innovations to increase the *World's* circulation, including illustrations, comic strips, a Sunday edition, and in 1887 an evening edition, the *Evening World*. In 1890, because of blindness and failing health, Pulitzer gave up the editorship of his papers, but he continued to direct their policies. When William Randolph Hearst (1863–1951) bought the New York *Journal* in 1895 and began to compete with the *World,* Pulitzer changed his editorial policies. He adopted the sensationalism of "yellow journalism," and between 1896 and 1898 both the *World* and the *Journal*—in a battle for readership—inflamed anti-Spanish sentiments that contributed to the outbreak of the Spanish-American War. The *World* later returned to its former high standards and became the nation's leading Democratic newspaper. After Joseph Pulitzer's death, his sons, Ralph Pulitzer (1879–1939) and Joseph Pulitzer (1885–1955), were the publishers of the *World* and *Evening World* until 1931, when they sold out to the Scripps-Howard newspaper group. The new owners discontinued the *World* and merged the *Evening World* with the *Telegram* to form the New York *World-Telegram*. In his will, the elder Pulitzer bequeathed the money for both the Columbia Graduate School of Journalism and the prizes that still bear his name. The prizes, ranging from $500 to $1,000, were first awarded in 1917.

R

REED, Thomas Brackett (1839–1902). A distinguished Maine-born lawyer and Republican politician, Reed was a powerful member of the House of Representatives for 22 years. As Speaker (1889–1891 and 1895–1899) of the House, he forced the adoption of the so-called Reed Rules, which increased the Speaker's power to secure the passage of legislation endorsed by the majority party. These rules enabled him to exercise autocratic powers and led to his nickname, Czar Reed. After graduating from Bowdoin College in Maine in 1860, Reed became a lawyer. He served in the Maine legislature (1868–1870) and as state attorney general (1870–1873) before entering the House of Representatives in 1877. In 1882, he was appointed to the committee on rules and began a fight for procedural reforms to end minority filibustering and enable the majority party to govern. His battle culminated

in the adoption of the Reed Rules in February, 1890. Reed was subsequently replaced as Speaker in 1891, and the rules were voided until he was re-elected to the Speakership four years later. Reed, who was a bitter enemy of imperialism, strongly opposed the war with Spain and the annexation of Hawaii in 1898. Disgusted with the direction of American foreign policy, he resigned from the House in September, 1899. He was a great debater and coined many witty epigrams and aphorisms, such as the definition of a statesman as "a successful politician who is dead." Some trace of the Reed Rules still remain in effect in the House.

RIIS, Jacob August (1849–1914). Riis was known as the great emancipator of the slums. A journalist, author, and reformer, he led a personal crusade to remedy the social ills afflicting New York's lower classes. Born in Ribe, Denmark, and educated by his father, Riis cleared a local tenement of rats at the age of 14.

Life magazine of 1904 depicted Jacob Riis as a "Bold Viking."

After serving as a carpenter's apprentice in Copenhagen, Riis immigrated to New York in 1870, where for the first few years he eked out a living by working variously as a farmer, a peddler, a brick maker, and a coal miner. In 1877, Riis was hired as a police reporter by the New York *Tribune,* and 11 years later, in the same capacity, he joined the New York *Evening Sun.* Assignments for stories on accidents and crime led Riis to witness the moral, spiritual, and physical degradation of the people in the city's ghettos, and he decided to do all he could to eliminate these conditions. His articles, lectures, and such books as *How the Other Half Lives* (1890) depicted the urban poor and exposed dens of filth and vice. The publicity was meant to shock a complacent public into providing relief for tenement dwellers. Through Riis' efforts, playgrounds and parks were introduced in blighted areas, the city's contaminated water supply was improved, child-labor laws were passed, and a school for truants was founded. In addition, Mulberry Bend, the worst slum in New York, was razed. It was replaced in the late 1880s by the Jacob A. Riis Neighborhood House for Social Work. Although Riis made many enemies—especially landlords and politicians—he also gained powerful allies, including Theodore Roosevelt (1858–1919), who as governor of New York and later as President offered Riis important government posts. He declined them all, saying that he was too busy.

RYDER, Albert Pinkham (1847–1917). One of America's greatest artists, Ryder painted landscapes, seascapes, still lifes, and symbolic pictures that are imbued with poetic qualities. Born in the then important whaling port of New Bedford, Massachusetts, Ryder was haunted by the sea throughout his life. A recurrent theme in his painting is a lonely ship on a moonlit sea. About 1870, Ryder settled in New York City, where, except for several short trips to Europe, he lived for the rest of his life. He often gave away his best paintings to his friends. He generally reworked his canvases numerous times, with the result that he completed only about 165 paintings. Because of many unsuccessful experiments with various oil paints, many of Ryder's canvases have deteriorated. His early paintings were landscapes, but about 1880 he began producing imaginative subjects based on Biblical or literary themes. The abstract treatment of his subjects give his paintings a quality that links him with the modern movement in art. Because of his popularity, Ryder was often copied, and forgeries of his works outnumber the genuine ones by a ratio of almost 5 to 1. Today, Ryder's works are in many leading museums and collections in the United States and Canada. Some of the most famous and characteristic examples of his art are the *Temple of the Mind* in the Albright-Knox Gallery, Buffalo, New York; *Death on a Pale Horse,* or *The Race Track* in the Cleveland Museum; *Toilers of the Sea* in the Metropolitan Museum of Art, New York City, and *The Flying Dutchman* in the National Museum of American Art, Washington, D.C.

S

SAINT-GAUDENS, Augustus (1848–1907). One of America's foremost sculptors, Saint-Gaudens created some of the most famous monuments of the late 19th and early 20th centuries. Saint-Gaudens was brought to the United States from his native Ireland as an infant and grew up in New York City. At the age of 13, he was apprenticed to a cameo cutter and also began attending evening classes in drawing at New York's Cooper Union. He later studied at the National Academy of Design, also in New York. Saint-Gaudens completed his artistic education in Paris, where he studied (1867–1870) at the Ecole des Beaux-Arts, and then in Rome (1870–1873), where he gained familiarity with neoclassicism and the art of the Italian Renaissance. While in Rome, he produced his first figure, *Hiawatha,* a marble version of which is in Saratoga, New York. Saint-Gaudens developed a style noted for its naturalism and vitality. He maintained a studio in New York City from 1873 to 1885, and then from 1885 until his death he worked in Cornish, New Hampshire. Saint-Gaudens first gained public acclaim in 1881 with a life-sized statue of Admiral David Glasgow Farragut (1801–1870) in New York City's Madison Square. The noted architect Stanford White (1853–1906) collaborated with him on its marble base. Later works included a statue of Deacon Samuel Chapin (1598–1675) known as *The Puritan,* which is in Springfield, Massachusetts; a statue of Abraham Lincoln (1809–1865) in Chicago's Lincoln Park; a memorial to Colonel Robert Gould Shaw (1837–1863) on Boston Common; and the equestrian statue of General John A. Logan (1826–1886) in Chicago. One of Saint-Gaudens' best-known works, completed in 1903, is the equestrian statue of another Civil War hero, General William Tecumseh

Saint-Gaudens' "Grief" decorates the monument to Mrs. Henry Adams.

Sherman (1820–1891), at the southeast entrance to Central Park in New York City. In 1891, Saint-Gaudens completed what is probably his most famous work, a monument to Mrs. Henry Adams, the wife of the historian **Henry Adams** (*see*). This memorial, which stands in Rock Creek Cemetery in Washington, D. C., is one of the most tragic sculptures of modern times, and its brooding central figure is often called "Grief." Adams, who had commissioned it, called the monument *The Peace of God.* The sculptor himself sometimes called the work *The Mystery of the Hereafter.* After his death, his house and studios at Cornish were opened to the public as the Augustus Saint-Gaudens Memorial.

SARGENT, John Singer (1856–1925). One of the greatest por-

Sargent was photographed with his famous portrait Madame X.

trait artists of his day, Sargent specialized in painting likenesses of fashionable people in America and abroad during the late 1800s and early 1900s. The son of wealthy American parents, Sargent was born in Florence, Italy. He showed an artistic talent at an early age and studied drawing at Florence's Academy of Fine Arts. In 1874, he attended the Ecole des Beaux-Arts in Paris and studied under Carolus Duran (1837–1917), a renowned portrait artist. He made his first visit to the United States in 1876. Traveling to Spain in 1879, Sargent was influenced by the swift brush strokes of the Spanish master Velazquez (1599–1660) and as a result produced one of his early masterpieces, *El Jaleo*. The work that made Sargent famous, as well as infamous, was painted in 1884. Entitled *Madame X*, it consisted of a full-length view of a beauty of the day named Madame Gautreau. This picture, which highlighted the low neckline of its subject's dress, created a scandal of such magnitude among Parisians that Sargent allegedly had to flee Paris. He settled in London, where he established his studio in 1885. There, Sargent's virtuoso brushwork and his ability to create flattering portraits made him highly popular among socialites and theater people. He was deluged with commissions. He executed the portrait (*see p. 980*) of **Isabella Stewart Gardner** (*see*) while on a visit to America in 1888. Two years later, Sargent was commissioned to paint mural decorations for the Boston Public Library. Deciding on the history of religion as a theme, Sargent traveled to Egypt in 1891 to do research. He installed the first portion of the work in the library in 1894 (the last was completed in 1916). After 1895, Sargent traveled to the United States almost annually, and in 1903 he established a studio in Boston. Although he spent most of his active career in England, he declined a British knighthood in 1907 on the ground that he was an American. After 1910, Sargent concentrated on painting in watercolors.

SAWYER, Philetus (1816–1900). A wealthy Wisconsin lumberman who dominated the Republican Party in his state for many years, Sawyer served in Congress for 22 years. He was a Representative from 1865 to 1875 and a Senator between 1881 and 1893. Born near Rutland, Vermont, and raised in Crown Point, New York, Sawyer received little formal education, but he thoroughly learned the lumberman's trade as a worker in pine forests. About 1847, he moved to the vicinity of Oshkosh, Wisconsin, where he soon amassed a fortune in the timber business and from railroad and banking investments. Sawyer served in the Wisconsin assembly (1857–1861) before being elected to the House of Representatives. He retired after five terms to attend to business interests but in 1880 sought and won election to the Senate, which at that time was virtually a "millionaires' club." Widely known as an advocate of rugged individualism, Sawyer saw his influence in Wisconsin politics decline sharply in the early 1890s after he was accused of trying to bribe a judge in connection with corruption charges against Republican state officials. The young progressive Republican Robert M. La Follette (1855–1925) helped break Sawyer's power as the party boss in Wisconsin. Defeated for reelection in 1892, Sawyer retired to his mansion in Oshkosh.

STANLEY, Henry Morton (1841–1904). The man who found the missing Dr. David Livingstone (1813–1873) and coined the expression "Dark Continent," Stanley is regarded as the most important pioneer explorer of Africa. Originally a roving journalist, Stanley reported on some of the most spectacular events of his day, including Indian campaigns in the West and wars in Spain, Crete, and Ethiopia. In 1869, he was commissioned by the New York *Herald* to search for Livingstone, a Scottish missionary, in central Africa. He arrived there in 1871, and after eight months of trekking through jungle and mountains, Stanley found the famous clergyman-explorer near Lake Tanganyika, on November 10, 1871, and greeted him with what has become the famous phrase, "Dr. Livingstone,

I presume?" Stanley's name at birth was John Rowlands. Born in Denbigh, Wales, he endured a bitter childhood. Unwanted by his parents or relatives, he was raised in a workhouse, where he was beaten by the schoolmaster. At the age of 15, he fled, first to Liverpool, England, and then to the United States. Arriving in New Orleans in 1859, he worked for a cotton merchant, who informally adopted him and whose name—Henry Morton Stanley—the youth took as his own. Stanley enlisted as a Confederate soldier at the outbreak of the Civil War in 1861 and was captured the following year at the Battle of Shiloh. After his release from prison, he joined the Union Army and later served in the Union Navy during 1864. Stanley became a newspaper correspondent about 1865 and, by the time of his trip to Africa in search of Livingstone, had established a considerable reputation. Stanley's growing interest in the exploration of Africa led him to make three expeditions to that continent between 1874 and 1889, during which he explored unmapped areas of the Congo and Nile Rivers, and Lakes Edward, Victoria, and Tanganyika. Representing King Leopold II (1835–1909) of Belgium, Stanley helped found the Congo Free State in the middle 1880s. He was known by the natives in the area as *Bula Matari*—meaning "the strong one," or "the rock-breaker"—because of his work building railroads. Although a naturalized American, Stanley was restored to British citizenship in 1892. He served in Parliament from 1895 to 1900.

STRONG, Josiah (1847–1916). A Congregational clergyman, Strong was a pioneer in the Christian Socialist movement of the late 19th century that tried to solve social and industrial problems through the teachings of Jesus. Strong first gained widespread acclaim in 1885 when he published *Our Country*, a sociological treatise that analyzed the evils of modern industrial society and challenged the Christian Church to help improve existing social conditions. In 1893, he published *The New Era,* in which he stated that the task of the Church was to extend, purify, and perpetuate the Kingdom of Christ on earth. Born in Illinois, Strong was educated at the Lane Theological Seminary in Cincinnati, Ohio, and was ordained pastor of a Congregational church in Cheyenne, Wyoming, in 1871. He later held several other Congregational pastorates. In 1898, Strong founded the League for Social Service, which was reorganized as the American Institute for Social Service four years later. This institute was designed to advance the cause of Christian Socialism, especially the theories outlined by Strong in his books. Strong also believed that the Anglo-Saxons had a "genius for colonization," and like **John Fiske** (*see*), he believed Americans were destined to control vast areas of the world because they were "the fittest."

SULLIVAN, John Lawrence (1858–1918). The heavyweight boxing champion of the world between 1882 and 1892, Sullivan was the best—as well as the most colorful—pugilist of his era. Born in Boston of Irish immigrant parents, Sullivan came by his size from his mother, a tall, 180-pound woman, and his belligerence from his father. After a grade-school education, he worked as a plumber and a tinsmith. He excelled at sports and was several times offered positions on professional baseball teams. Sullivan began boxing at 19 and was soon giving exhibitions in the Boston area. In 1880, he offered to fight "any man breathing," including Paddy Ryan, the heavyweight champion. Two years later, on February 7, in a bareknuckle match on the turf at Mississippi City, Mississippi, Sullivan knocked out Ryan to become the champion. He quickly became a popular

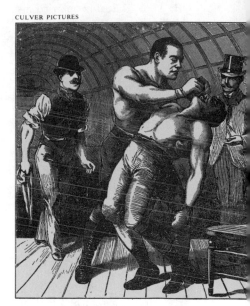

Sullivan wiped off Paddy Ryan's brow after knocking him out in 1882.

hero and mingled with dignitaries in America and Europe. The city of Boston gave him a diamond-studded belt in 1887. Despite frequent drinking bouts that bloated his 5-foot-10 inch, 180-pound frame, "The Boston Strong Boy" remained undefeated for 10 years. In 1889, he beat Jake Kilrain by a decision after 75 rounds in the broiling Mississippi sun in the last bareknuckle championship fight. Sullivan was the chief proponent in the United States of adoption of the Marquess of Queensbury rules, and on September 7, 1892, fighting with gloves under the newly adopted rules, he was pummeled senseless in the 21st round by the agile James J. "Gentleman Jim" Corbett (1866–1933). When he regained his wits, Sullivan told Corbett, "I fought once too often, but I am glad that the championship remains in America." Sullivan then became, in turn, an actor, a saloon operator, and a lecturer on the evils of drink. In 1908, after divorcing a chorus girl, Annie Bates, he married his childhood sweetheart, Kate Harkins. They retired to a farm in Massachusetts in 1912.

SULLIVAN, Louis (1856–1924). Known as the father of modernism in architecture, Sullivan was the leading designer of the so-called Chicago school of architecture. After he had studied at the Massachusetts Institute of Technology (1872–1873), Sullivan took a job in Chicago with the architectural firm of **William L. Jenney** (see), the creator of the first steel-frame skyscraper. In 1874, the young architect left for Paris, where he resumed his studies at the Ecole des Beaux-Arts. He soon returned to Chicago and established a reputation as a draftsman. In 1879, Sullivan joined the firm of Dankmar Adler (1844–1900). Two years later the company changed its name to Adler and Sullivan. Sullivan developed an architectural style based on the principle that "form follows function." He believed that the exterior of a building should reflect its interior function. A modernist, Sullivan abandoned the Romanesque style of the 1880s and later opposed the classical revival of the 1890s. His departure from the Romanesque was first evident in the interior design of Chicago's Auditorium Building, which was completed in 1890. With its excellent acoustics and delicate ornamentation, the building earned the firm an international reputation. Sullivan then adopted the newly conceived method of steel-skeleton construction in his Wainwright Building in St. Louis, which his protégé, Frank Lloyd Wright (1869–1959), called "the master key to the skyscraper as Architecture the world over." Insisting that American architects develop their own style and not try to copy European models, Sullivan was the only architect to design an original building not in the classical style for the Chicago World's Columbian Exposition in 1893 (see pp. 974–975). With the death of Adler in 1900, the work of the firm dwindled. Thereafter, Sullivan designed a number of small banks throughout the Midwest. In 1924, he published *The Autobiography of An Idea,* an exposition of his thesis that form follows function.

T

TALMAGE, Thomas De Witt (1832–1902). A New Jersey-born Presbyterian clergyman, editor, and lecturer, Talmage was one of the most popular preachers in America in the 1870s, when he was minister of the Central Presbyterian Church in Brooklyn. His sermons were published weekly in nearly 3,500 newspapers. After graduating from the New Brunswick Theological Seminary in 1856, Talmage was pastor of the Dutch Reformed Church in Belleville, New Jersey, until 1859. He then spent four years at a church in Syracuse, New York, before he was called to the Second Dutch Reformed Church in Philadelphia in 1862. There, he first gained widespread acclaim for his sensational sermons in which, among other things, he condemned card playing, Mormonism, and strong drinks. In 1869, Talmage became minister of the Central Presbyterian Church in Brooklyn. He attracted such huge audiences that in 1870 the congregation built him a new church called the Tabernacle. It burned down two years later in one of the worst fires in the history of Brooklyn. Two other Tabernacles were constructed subsequently, but they too were destroyed by fire. Although Talmage was extremely popular, he also had many critics, who called him a "pulpit clown" and a fraud. In 1879, the Brooklyn Presbytery accused him "of falsehood and deceit, and... using improper methods of preaching, which tend to bring religion into contempt." Talmage, however, was acquitted and continued to preach at the church there. He served his last pastorate (1894–1899) at the First Presbyterian Church of Washington, D. C. Talmage edited the *Christian at Work* (1874–1876), *Frank Leslie's Sunday Magazine* (1881–1889), and after 1890, the *Christian Herald.* In addition, he lectured widely in both America and England and published many volumes of sermons. His autobiography, *T. De Witt Talmage as I Knew Him* (1912), was completed after his death by his wife.

TAYLOR, Bayard (1825–1878). Restless and adventurous by nature, Taylor was a writer and lecturer whose wide travels throughout the world were the subject of numerous, fascinating books. Taylor began writing poetry at the age of seven and published his first volume of verse, *Ximena,* in 1844 while apprenticed to a printer in his native Pennsylvania. That same year, Taylor was commissioned by three publications to travel throughout Europe. He hiked across most of the Continent and sent back his observations, which were published in the New York *Tribune,* the *Saturday Evening Post,* and the *United States Gazette.* Upon his return two years later, Taylor's letters were collected in book form, *Views Afoot* (1846). Taylor joined the staff of the *Tribune* in 1848. He was sent the following year to cover the gold rush in California. He recorded his visit to the mining regions in *Eldorado* (1850). Taylor set out in 1851 to travel through Europe, Central Africa, Egypt, Syria, Turkey, India, Japan, and China. While in Shanghai two years later, he briefly joined the fleet of Commodore Matthew C. Perry (1794–1858). After his return to America, Taylor described his adventures in *A Journey to Central Africa* (1854), *A Visit to India, China, and Japan* (1855), and *The Lands of the Saracen* (1855). Through these books and the lectures he gave throughout the nation, Taylor became a modern Marco Polo to countless Americans. In 1856, the author again sailed for Europe. Out of his two-year tour came three more travel books. During the Civil War, Taylor was a correspondent for the *Tribune* in Washington, D. C., and later secretary of the United States legation in St. Petersburg, Russia (1862–1863). In the early 1870s, his translation of *Faust,* by the German poet Johann Wolfgang von Goethe (1749–1832), earned him a nonresident professorship at Cornell University. From 1870 until 1877, Taylor lectured occasionally on German literature while writing poetry and several minor novels. In 1878, he was appointed United States minister to Germany. He died later the same year in Berlin and was buried in Pennsylvania.

TILTON, Theodore (1835–1907). Tilton ruined a promising career as a newspaper editor by becoming involved in a lawsuit against the famous preacher Henry Ward Beecher (1813–1887). Born in New York City, Tilton gained reporting experience working on the New York *Tribune* and the New York *Observer,* on which he was assigned to record in shorthand Beecher's sermons at the Plymouth Church in Brooklyn. There, he met a Sunday-school teacher, Elizabeth Richards, and married her in 1855. The following year, Tilton joined the staff of the *Independent,* a Congregationalist journal, and from 1862 to 1871 he served as its editor. Meanwhile, Tilton had become a close friend of Beecher's and enlisted the minister's aid in making the *Independent* into an organ of political power, promoting emancipation, an anti-Southern Radical Republican policy of Reconstruction, and women's suffrage. Then, in the summer of 1870, Tilton's wife confessed to him that she had had intimate relations with Beecher. Although Beecher denied Tilton's accusation of adultery and Tilton initially tried to shield his wife from publicity, the triangle inevitably became the subject of gossip. Tilton was dismissed from the *Independent* in 1871, and the following year the scandal finally broke in a newspaper. Tilton formally lodged charges of adultery against Beecher and sued him for $100,000 in damages. The Plymouth congregation remained steadfastly loyal to their pastor, and Elizabeth Tilton left her husband and rallied to Beecher's defense. The trial, beginning on January 11, 1875, and lasting 112 trial days, resulted in a hung jury. Four years after the trial, Mrs. Tilton recanted and pronounced her husband's allega-

tions correct. The couple never reconciled. His reputation and finances ruined, Tilton left America in 1883, finally settling in Paris, where he lived the rest of his life, writing books, poems, and articles.

TWAIN, Mark (1835–1910). The first major American author to use colloquial rather than "proper" language in his writings, Twain was essentially an entertainer and a humorist. Called by **William Dean Howells** (*see*) "the Lincoln of our literature," he also was a reformer and a tireless enemy of political, religious, and social stupidities and hypocrisies. "Against the assault of laughter," he said, "nothing can stand." Born Samuel Langhorne Clemens, Twain grew up in Hannibal, Missouri, on the Mississippi River. His boyhood experiences furnished him with the material for *The Adventures of Tom Sawyer* (1876) and his masterpiece, *Adventures of Huckleberry Finn* (1884), the story of a backwoods boy and a runaway slave. Twain's father died in 1847, and the youth dropped out of school to work as a printer's apprentice. He left Hannibal in 1853 and for the next four years worked as a printer in St. Louis, New York, Philadelphia, and other cities. Twain began work on a riverboat on the Mississippi in 1857 and became a river pilot two years later. Such works as *Life on the Mississippi* (1883) stemmed from this period, as did his literary pseudonym (in riverboat jargon, *mark twain* means "two fathoms deep" and signifies safe water). Twain went west in 1861 —later recording the experience in *Roughing It* (1872)—to the Nevada Territory, where he worked as a secretary to his brother, a minor government offi-

Mark Twain

cial. He prospected without success for silver and then became a journalist in Virginia City. Continuing newspaper work in California after 1864, Twain first won wide attention with the publication in a New York newspaper in 1865 of a frontier "tall tale" about a jumping frog. As "The Celebrated Jumping Frog of Calaveras County," this story became the title piece for his first book, which appeared in 1867. After visiting the Sandwich Islands (Hawaii) in 1866, Twain turned to giving humorous lectures in the fashion of Artemus Ward (1834–1867). His trip to Europe and the Holy Land in 1867 supplied material for *The Innocents Abroad* (1869), which earned him a national reputation. Twain married Olivia Langdon (1837–1904) of Elmira, New York, in 1870 and two years later settled down to be "respectable" in Hartford, Connecticut. *The Prince and the Pauper* (1882), *A Tramp Abroad* (1880), and *A Connecticut Yankee at King Arthur's Court* (1889), as well as

Tom Sawyer and *Huckleberry Finn*, were among works that appeared in the next two decades, and they brought him a large income. However, investments in unsound printing and publishing ventures forced him to go on a lecture tour (1895–1896) around the world to raise money to pay his debts. Personal suffering in his later years, especially the death of his wife and two of his daughters, increasingly turned Twain's humor to bitter satire and diminished his once boundless zest for life. *The Tragedy of Pudd'nhead Wilson* (1894), *The Man That Corrupted Hadleyburg* (1900), *What is Man?* (1906), and *The Mysterious Stranger* (published posthumously in 1916) reflect this pessimism.

TWEED, William Marcy ("Boss") (1823–1878). This infamous Tammany Hall leader's control of the Democratic Party in New York in the 1860s led to an unsurpassed amount of corruption and gave a bad name to organized politics. After working as a bookkeeper in his father's brush factory, Tweed became a volunteer fireman in 1848 and two years later was elected foreman of his firehouse. In 1851, he was elected alderman and a year later elected to the House of Representatives. Preferring municipal politics, Tweed returned to the city council after just one term in Congress. In 1856, he was elected to the board of supervisors, which had been established to check corrupt election practices. Tweed gained control of the board and made political appointments to ensure his own power. He himself, at various times, was school commissioner, commissioner of public works, and a state senator. In addition, he was the grand sa-

chem (head) of Tammany Hall, the Democratic political club. Both the governor of the state and the mayor of New York City owed their positions to him. In addition, Boss Tweed—as he was called by his opponents— controlled a number of businesses, including a furniture company that sold $50 sofas to the city for $5,000 apiece, and a street-cleaning company that was paid enormous sums by the city, despite the fact that it never cleaned the streets and did not even own a broom. His grandest plan for robbing the city treasury was the New York County Courthouse, begun in 1868 at an estimated cost of $500,000. The final cost was $12,000,000, at least two-thirds of which went into the pockets of Tweed and his friends. It is estimated that the Tweed Ring stole between $45,000,000 and $200,000,000 from the city between 1869 and 1871 alone. In 1870, the cartoonist Thomas Nast (1840–1902) of *Harper's Weekly* and George Jones (1811–1891), a founder of the New York *Times,* began exposing Tweed's fraudulent practices. Tweed tried unsuccessfully to buy their silence, but in October, 1871, he was arrested on civil charges of misappropriating city funds. A bail of $2,000,-000 was set, which Tweed paid. That December, criminal charges of fraud were brought against him, and in November, 1873, he was convicted and sentenced to 12 years in prison. The court of appeals reduced his sentence to a year. Shortly after his release, Tweed again was arrested on civil charges, this time brought by the state. Tweed escaped when he was allowed to visit his family. He fled first to Cuba and then to Spain. Spanish authorities, using a Nast cartoon to identify him, found Tweed and extradited him to America in 1876. Hoping for a light sentence, Tweed, whose health was failing, talked openly of many of his corrupt dealings. He died in jail before going on trial.

V

VICTORIA (1819–1901). Queen of Great Britain and Ireland and Empress of India, Victoria ruled for 63 years, seven months, two days—the longest reign in English history. In the English-speaking world, she became the symbol of the Victorian Age, which was characterized by a preoccupation with respectability. Victoria succeeded to the throne on June 20, 1837, when her uncle, King William IV (1765–1837), died without an immediate heir. In the first few years of her reign, Victoria seemed to enjoy late-hour social activities, but this changed in 1840 when she married her German first cousin Prince Albert of Saxe-Coburg-Gotha (1819–1861). Victoria bore him nine children and became immersed in the responsibilities of family life. Albert, who was named Prince Consort in 1857, exercised such an influence on the queen that some critics referred to her as Queen Albertine. Shy, studious, and conservative, Albert is credited with setting the tone of the Victorian Age. Royal dinner parties, rather than being amusing, became examples of decorum. It was Albert who masterminded the great Crystal Palace Exhibition of 1851 as a means of promoting the arts and sciences of the Industrial Revolution to the increasingly affluent British public. The exhibition sparked a desire among the middle and upper classes for ornate possessions, particularly for the

home (*see pp. 947–957*). When Albert died in 1861, Victoria was so distraught that she did not appear in public for three years. In 1887 and 1897, jubilees were held to celebrate the 50th and 60th years of her reign, respectively. Because of its emphasis on superficial respectability, the Victorian Age has come to symbolize hypocrisy and narrow-mindedness. However, Victoria's conscientiousness and high moral standards helped to restore the prestige of the British crown after the reigns of several extravagant, irresponsible monarchs.

W

WALLACE, Lewis ("Lew") (1827–1905). Wallace, who is perhaps best known for writing the novel *Ben Hur,* was a Union general in the Civil War. The son of an Indiana governor, Wallace raised a company of infantry for the Mexican War and afterward practiced law in Indiana. During the Civil War, Wallace organized troops in his home state and in 1862 led forces in Virginia and Tennessee. The next year, he defended Cincinnati against Confederate attacks, and in 1864 he successfully blocked a raid on Washington, D. C. After the war, Wallace served on the court-martial board that tried the assassins of President Abraham Lincoln (1809–1865) and was president of the court that convicted Henry Wirz (?–1865), the commander of the notorious Confederate prison at Andersonville, Georgia. Wallace later was the governor (1878–1881) of the New Mexico Territory and then became the United States minister to Turkey (1881–1885). As an author, Wallace won an early reputation in 1873 for his novel *The Fair God,*

which dealt with the conquest of Mexico. However, it was *Ben Hur,* published in 1880, that gained him lasting fame. The novel, which dealt with the life of a Jewish prince during the time of Jesus Christ, sold more than 300,000 copies in its first 10 years. Since its publication, *Ben Hur* has been translated into many languages and has been turned into a stage play and two motion pictures. Wallace continued writing until his death. But none of his works ever achieved the enduring popularity that *Ben Hur* has enjoyed.

WALTERS, Henry (1848–1931). A wealthy Baltimore-born railroad magnate. Walters enlarged the art collection begun by his father, William Thompson Walters (1820–1894), who had made a fortune in railroads. In 1907, Henry Walters built the Walters Art Gallery in Baltimore to house the family collection, and two years later he opened it to public. At his death, he left the gallery and its contents to the city of Baltimore, together with one-fourth of his estate as an endowment. Walters first became acquainted with the art world during the Civil War, when he lived in Paris with his father. He then returned to America and graduated from Georgetown University in Washington, D. C., in 1869. He received a Master of Arts degree from Georgetown two years later and a Bachelor of Science degree from the Lawrence Scientific School of Harvard University in 1873. Walters then returned to Paris for two more years of study. While abroad, Walters increased his familiarity with artists and art dealers and began making additions to his father's collection. In America, he expanded his father's railroad holdings and became one of the richest men in the South. Walters made annual art-buying trips to Europe, where he acquired paintings, prints, sculpture, jewelry, textiles, watches, and illuminated manuscripts, as well as a large art library.

WARNER, Charles Dudley (1829–1900). A noted Massachusetts-born essayist, editor, and novelist, Warner collaborated with his friend **Mark Twain** (*see*) to write *The Gilded Age* (1873), the novel that gave its name to the last three decades of the 19th century in American history. Warner graduated from Hamilton College in 1851, delivering the commencement address, which he published as *The Book of Eloquence* (1851). After working as a railroad surveyor in Missouri, he became a lawyer in 1858. He practiced for two years in Chicago, before he abandoned law for a journalistic and literary career. In 1860, he moved to Hartford, Connecticut, where he was editor of the *Evening Press* from 1861 until 1867, when it merged with the Hartford *Courant*. Warner was associate editor and publisher of the *Courant* for the rest of his life. In 1871, he published his first collection of essays, *My Summer in a Garden*. This volume was followed by many other collections of gracefully written and humorous essays, including *Backlog Studies* (1873), *Being a Boy* (1878), and *On Horseback* (1888). Among other works, Warner also wrote literary criticism, many travel books, and a trilogy of novels—*A Little Journey in the World* (1889), *The Golden House* (1895), and *That Fortune* (1899)—that describes the gain and loss of a vast fortune. He was president of the National Institute of Arts and Letters.

WASHINGTON, Booker Taliaferro (1856–1915). Born a slave on a Virginia plantation, this black educator (*see p. 961*) sought the betterment of his race through vocational training and tried to achieve harmonious relations with the white world. Booker was the son of a mulatto slave mother and a white father. After the Civil War, he moved with his family to Malden, West Virginia, where he worked in salt furnaces and coal mines and was able to attend school. He adopted the surname of Washington, because, as he explained, it made him feel "equal to the situation." Washington studied for three years at Virginia's Hampton Institute, a black vocational school. He graduated in 1875 as a brick mason. Four years later, he became an instructor there in charge of the night school. In 1881, Washington was chosen by Samuel C. Armstrong (1839–1893), a white philanthropist and educator who had founded Hampton Institute, to establish an industrial and professional school for black students in Tuskegee, Alabama, which was named Tuskegee Institute. Believing that economic independence would be the means through which black people would eventually achieve social and political equality, Washington worked for the next 34 years to teach his students the virtues of self-reliance, industry, and thrift. At his death, Tuskegee was a thriving institution with more than 100 buildings, over 1,500 students, a faculty of about 200, and an endowment of nearly $2,000,000. From 1884 on, Washington traveled throughout the nation and in Europe, delivering lectures on behalf of Tuskegee Institute. In his most famous and controversial speech, delivered at the Atlanta Exposition on September 18, 1895, Washington asked the white community for aid in educating blacks. As a temporary measure, he said he favored segregation until blacks were economically indispensable to American industry. Washington thrust up his hand, declaring, "In all things that are purely social we can be as separate as the fingers, yet one as the hand in all things essential to mutual progress." Washington, whose conservative racial views had often been attacked by militant black intellectuals, became more tolerant of social protest in the early 1900s, and he supported other black leaders in their agitation for civil rights. His moderation made him the spokesman of his race before Presidents and industrialists, and he won many legislative grants and contributions to his cause. He wrote two autobiographical works, *Up From Slavery* (1901) and *My Larger Education* (1911).

WHARTON, Edith Newbold Jones (1862–1937). A famous novelist and short-story writer, Mrs. Wharton often described the upper-class society in which she had been raised. Two such novels were *The House of Mirth* (1905) and *The Age of Innocence* (1920), which won the Pulitzer Prize for fiction in 1921. However, her most famous novel, *Ethan Frome* (1911), a story of rural New England, was her least characteristic work. Mrs. Wharton was born into a wealthy and socially prominent New York family and was privately educated in the United States and Europe. She became an admirer of the writer **Henry James** (*see*). She revealed her admiration for James' fiction in many of her works, among them *The Old Maid,* one of four novelettes published under the title *Old New York* (1924). Like James, Mrs.

Wharton depicted the conflict of ethical values in New York society of the second half of the 19th century. Among her early works are several collections of short stories—*The Greater Inclination* (1899), *Crucial Instances* (1901), and *The Descent of Man* (1904) —the novelettes *The Touchstone* (1900) and *Sanctuary* (1903), and her first major novel, *The Valley of Decision* (1902), a historical tale set in 18th-century Italy. Married in 1885 to a wealthy Bostonian, Edward Wharton, she divorced him in 1913, six years after they had settled in Paris. It was in Paris that she wrote *Ethan Frome*. Set in rural New England, it is the tragic story of a man caught in a triangular love affair and is the first novel that Mrs. Wharton did not set against a background of affluence and high society. *The Custom of the Country* (1913) was reminiscent of Henry James because it described the moral and social conflicts of an American living in France. In 1922, Mrs. Wharton published *The Glimpses of the Moon,* an international novel of manners. In all, she wrote more than 50 novels. *Hudson River Bracketed* (1929) and its sequel, *The Gods Arrive* (1932), are important examples of the way she dealt with the contrasting cultural values of the Middle West, New York, England, and the Continent. Later collections of short stories include *Xingu and Other Stories* (1916), *Certain People* (1930), and *Ghosts* (1937). In addition, Mrs. Wharton wrote poetry, travel books, a volume of literary criticism entitled *The Writing of Fiction* (1925), and an autobiography, *A Backward Glance* (1934). She was awarded a cross of the French Legion of Honor for her relief work in Paris during World War I.

While living in London in 1885, Whistler posed for William Chase.

WHISTLER, James Abbott McNeill (1834–1903). Whistler was a leading American artist who is best remembered for a portrait of his mother, *Arrangement in Gray and Black,* which is popularly known as *Whistler's Mother.* Born in Massachusetts, Whistler lived for six years as a child in St. Petersburg, Russia, where his father, an engineer, was supervising the building of a railroad. After the death of his father in 1849, Whistler and his mother returned home, and two years later he enrolled as a cadet at West Point. He was dismissed in 1854 for disciplinary reasons and for failing a chemistry examination. Always a great wit, Whistler remarked later that "had silicon been a gas, I would have been a major general." Already appreciated for his artistic abilities, Whistler went to work for the United States Coast Survey as a draftsman. After a year, he decided to devote himself entirely to art. In 1855, he moved to Paris, where he studied with Charles Gleyre (1808–1874) and was influenced by the works of Hilaire Degas (1834–

1917) and Ignace Fantin-Latour (1836–1904). Whistler's first painting, *At the Piano,* was exhibited at the Royal Academy five years later. His first series of etchings, *French Set,* also appeared during his stay in Paris. Whistler made frequent trips to London during the early 1860s. His collection of etchings of the Thames River date from this period. In 1863, his portrait, *The White Girl,* was shown at the Salon des Refuses. The same year, Whistler established permenent residence in London. There, the painter became an admirer of Oriental art, and his work from 1864 to the end of the decade reflects a Japanese influence. During the 1870s, Whistler concentrated on full-length portraits. The picture of his mother, the portrait of British historian Thomas Carlyle (1795–1881) and that of a Miss Alexander were all painted in 1872. Together, the three pictures constitute perhaps his greatest contribution to painting. An outspoken, irreverent individual, Whistler was an artist who was little understood by most of his generation. Opposed to the "literary" painting of his time, he believed in "art for art's sake" and insisted that the subject of a painting was of little importance. When, in 1878, John Ruskin (1818–1900), an influential British critic, wrote that he "never expected to hear a coxcomb ask 200 guineas for flinging a pot of paint in the public's face," Whistler sued for libel. He won the case, but his reputation declined thereafter. The artist subsequently moved to Venice in 1879, where he produced his most brilliantly executed series of etchings. He returned to London a year later and for some time made lithographs. Among the books Whistler wrote were *Ten*

O'Clock (1888)—an exposition of his theories on art—and *The Gentle Art of Making Enemies* (1890).

WHITMAN, Walt (1819–1892). A poet who celebrated American democracy, the common man, and individualism, Whitman is ranked among America's greatest poets. Born Walter Whitman on Long Island, he left school at the age of 11 and the next year began work as a printer's devil. Early in 1846, Whitman assumed the editorship of the Brooklyn *Daily Eagle*. He was fired two years later for taking a strong antislavery stand. Whitman then worked intermittently for several newspapers while preparing *Leaves of Grass,* a book of poems published at his own expense in 1855. In all, 10 editions appeared during his lifetime, each one revised and containing more poems than the previous one. Whitman's undisguised references to the body and sex caused him to be denounced as the "dirtiest beast of his age." His poems also departed from the traditional verse form. Instead, he employed free verse in long rythmical lines. For example, "Song of Myself," the first poem in *Leaves of Grass* and typical of his reverence for his fellow man, begins, *"I celebrate myself, and sing myself,/ And what I assume you shall assume,/ For every atom belonging to me as good belongs to you."* In response to the Confederate shelling of Fort Sumter, South Carolina, in 1861, Whitman wrote "Beat! Beat! Drums!" —the first of a collection of poems published after the Civil War in *Drum-Taps*. Other poems dealing with the Civil War and its aftermath were "O Captain! My Captain!" and "When Lilacs Last in the Dooryard Bloom'd," both tributes to Abraham Lincoln

Copies of this 1887 photo of Walt Whitman were sold to raise money for him.

(1809–1861), one of Whitman's greatest heroes. The latter poem is considered one of the finest poems of mourning in world literature. Whitman nursed wounded soldiers in Washington, D. C., during the war and remained there afterward as a clerk in the Department of the Interior. He was dismissed in June, 1865, when it was discovered that he was the author of *Leaves of Grass*. However, friends soon helped him secure another clerkship in the Attorney General's office. While working there, Whitman published in 1871 *Democratic Vistas,* a prose work. He frankly expressed his disillusionment with American democracy but remained convinced that the

people possessed a "miraculous wealth of latent power and capacity." In 1873, Whitman suffered a stroke and left Washington, D. C. He lived with his brother in Camden, New Jersey, remaining there until his death 19 years later. During that period, he worked on revising *Leaves of Grass,* wrote some articles, and lectured.

WILLARD, Frances Elizabeth (1839–1898). A social reformer, Miss Willard was a founder of the **Woman's Christian Temperance Union** (*see*) and played a major role in the campaign for the prohibition of liquor. Born in upstate New York, she spent her childhood in Ohio and Wisconsin.

Miss Willard attended the Milwaukee Female College about 1856 and then went to Northwestern Female College in Evanston, Illinois, from which she graduated in 1859. An adamant believer in female independence, she never married. She taught school and served as president of the Evanston College for Ladies from 1871 to 1874. That year, a national crusade for temperance was getting under way. Groups of women were appearing on streets and invading saloons, singing hymns and praying for the salvation of those addicted to liquor. Miss Willard joined one of these groups in Pittsburgh and delivered her first public prayer, kneeling in the sawdust of a Market Street saloon. She subsequently became head of the Chicago W.C.T.U., was elected president of the national organization in 1879, and presided over the world W.C.T.U. in 1891. In addition, Miss Willard helped to organize the Prohibition Party in 1882, lectured throughout the United States, and wrote many articles on prohibition. Unlike the more militant **Carrie Nation** (*see*), she never resorted to wrecking saloons to promote temperance.

WISTER, Owen (1860–1938). A novelist, short-story writer, and biographer, Wister wrote *The Virginian,* perhaps the most famous Western novel of its day. It sold more than 1,500,000 copies during Wister's lifetime and was adapted for the Broadway stage, as well as for the motion-picture screen. Wister was born in Germantown, Pennsylvania. His father was a well-known physician, and his mother was the daughter of the noted British actress Fanny Kemble (1809–1893). Many persons of eminence, including the novelist

Henry James (*see*), were frequent visitors at the Wister home. After schooling at private academies in Europe and America, Wister attended Harvard, graduating *summa cum laude* in 1882. One of his college classmates and a lifelong friend was Theodore Roosevelt (1858–1919). Wister studied music in Europe for two years before entering the Harvard Law School in 1885. On his doctor's advice, he began spending his summers on Wyoming ranches. He was admitted to the Philadelphia bar in 1889, but intrigued by his experiences in Wyoming, he resolved to tell in fiction the story of the West. Three collections of his stories, *Red Men and White* (1896), *Lin McLean* (1898), and *The Jimmyjohn Boss* (1900) preceded the publication of *The Virginian* (1902), which met with immediate acclaim. With its magnificent descriptions of the Western terrain, its pretty, schoolteacher heroine, and its soft-spoken but tough hero, the book did much to further the myth of the romantic life of the cowboy. Such clichés as "When you call me that, *smile!*" derive from *The Virginian*. Wister also wrote biographies of Presidents George Washington (1732–1799), Ulysses S. Grant (1822–1885), and his friend Theodore Roosevelt, as well as children's books, satires, and farces. A political conservative, Wister spent the last part of his life opposing the liberal policies of Presidents Woodrow Wilson (1856–1924) and Franklin D. Roosevelt (1882–1945).

WOMAN'S CHRISTIAN TEMPERANCE UNION. Dedicated to ending the production and consumption of alcoholic beverages, the W.C.T.U. became an important force in national life during

the late 1800s. A new phase of this temperance movement, which dated back to the colonial period, had begun in late 1873. Inspired by a lecture given by a health authority, women in Hillsboro, Ohio, embarked on a crusade to close the town's saloons. The campaign soon spread to other communities, and within two months the sale and serving of liquor had ceased—without laws being passed—in nearly 20 states. Despite these successes, temperance advocates realized that their achievements might be temporary, so they decided to form a permanent organization to wage the war against alcohol. The W.C.T.U. was officially formed at a national convention of temperance women from 17 states, held at Cleveland, Ohio, in November, 1874. Under the leadership of **Frances Willard** (*see*), the W.C.T.U. grew rapidly from 1879 to 1898, becoming international in scope by 1891 and giving rise to an offshoot, the Anti-Saloon League, in 1893. Relying mainly on moral suasion to convince people, the W.C.T.U. painted grim pictures of the saloon as the destroyer of home and family and the path to corruption and crime. The W.C.T.U. also sponsored programs advocating, among other things, prison reform, women's suffrage, and world peace. Because of its efforts, every state required temperance instruction in its public schools by 1900, and many of the children thus taught favored the enactment of prohibition later when they were adults. The W.C.T.U. and its activities have continued into the present day and now include campaigns against vice and the sale of harmful drugs. There is a chapter of the organization in nearly every state, territory, and dependency of the United States.